MANUAL OF THE

Waffen-SS

Badges, Uniforms, Equipment

by
Walther-Karl Holzmann

Black and white drawings
by D.S.V. Fosten
Colour art by R.J. Marrion

BELLONA PUBLICATIONS

**BELLONA PUBLICATIONS
ARGUS BOOKS LTD**
14 ST JAMES ROAD,
WATFORD, HERTS

First published 1976

ISBN 0 85242 487 6 (limp cover edition)

Printed in Great Britain
by ◎ Edwin Snell printers

Introduction

THIS book attempts to provide as much information as possible in visual form, either in photographs, or in drawings, on the uniforms, badges and head dress of the SS-Verfügungstruppe and the Waffen-SS. It is a simple manual for those who wish to easily identify badges, uniforms and specialised clothing without delving too deeply into the very elaborate and complicated structure, heirarchy and order of battle of the various formations. Those readers who do wish to research further into the subject are advised to read the definitive multi-volume work on the SS by Andrew Mollo published by the Historical Research Unit, Dr Wolf Keilig's comprehensive study of the formations and orders of battle of the Wehrmacht and the Waffen-SS in his massive work the *Des Deutschen Heeres 1939-1945* in several volumes, Dr Klietmann's part work on Waffen-SS formations and insignia, Beadle and Hartmann's *Divisions, Abzeichen der Waffen-SS, The Waffen-SS, Its Uniforms, Insignia and Equipment 1938-45* by Fosten and Marrion and the several volume work by Bender. A history of the Waffen-SS is not given. This will be found in the works mentioned above.

In brief Waffen-SS units were formed as follows:

English	*German*
Division	Division
Brigade	Brigade
Regiment	Standarte
Battalion	Sturmbann
Company	Sturm
Platoon	Zug
Section	Gruppe

A regiment comprised three battalions. The battalion had four companies and each company three platoons. Each platoon had four sections.

The true Germanic Divisions were prefixed with the letters 'SS'; Volksdeutsche and foreign formations contained the words 'Waffen' or 'Freiwilligen'. Component regiments were similarly easily identified — for example in the 29th *Waffen* Grenadier Division der SS (Italien) the infantry *regiments* were SS *Waffen* Grenadier Regiments 71, 72 and 73 and similarly in the 30th *Waffen* Grenadier Division der SS (Russisches Nr.2) we find the SS *Waffen* Grenadier Regiments 75, 76 and 77.

It should also be noted that from 1942-1943 a system of naming Waffen-SS ranks to relate more closely with Wehrmacht structuring was introduced. Thereafter a private in a Panzer Regiment became an SS Panzerschutze and an SS cavalry trooper an SS Reiter, etc.

Thanks are extended to Theodor Hartmann, L. Milner, R. Marrion and Brian Davis for their help in providing photographs and to David Littlejohn who provided some of the information on badges.

The camouflage helmet cover and smock being worn in 1940 by a man of SS-Regiment "Der Führer". His tunic is the first pattern SS field grey blouse issued in 1939.

Officer of heavy artillery, SS-Standarte "Germania", October 1940, wearing the first pattern SS field grey blouse and the early pattern collar patch with regimental number. Note helmet insignia.

CONTENTS

Colour plates: I — selection of flags and banners, II — camouflage clothing patterns, III — national legion sleeve badges, IV — national legion badges and rank insignia for camouflage clothing.

Waffen-SS Units

Armee

5. SS Panzer Armee

Armee Korps

SS General Kommando
SS Panzer-Generalkommando
SS Panzer Armeekorps
I. SS Panzer Armee Korps
II. SS Panzer Armee Korps
III. (Germanisches) SS Panzer Armee Korps
IV. SS Panzer Armee Korps
V. SS Gebirgs Armee Korps
VI. (Lettisches) SS Freiwilligen Armee Korps
IX. Waffen-Gebirgs (SS) Armee Korps
XI. SS Armee Korps
XII. SS Armee Korps
XIV. SS Armee Korps
XV. SS Armee Korps
XVIII. SS Armee Korps
XV. (SS) Kosaken-Kavallerie Korps

Divisions

1. SS Panzer "Leibstandarte Adolf Hitler" Division
2. SS Panzer Division "Das Reich"
3. SS Panzer Division "Totenkopf"
4. SS Polizei-Panzergrenadier Division
5. SS Panzer Division "Wiking"
6. SS Gebirgs Division "Nord"
7. SS Freiwilligen-Gebirgs Division "Prinz Eugen"
8. SS Kavalleriedivision "Florian Geyer"
9. SS Panzer Division "Hohenstaufen"
10. SS Panzer Division "Frundsberg"
11. SS Freiwilligen Panzergrenadierdivision "Nordland"
12. SS Panzer Division "Hitler Jugend"
13. Waffen Gebirgs Division der SS "Handschar" (Kroatisches Nr.1)
14. Waffen Grenadier Division der SS (Galicisches Nr.1)
15. Waffen Grenadier Division der SS (Lettisches Nr.1)
16. SS Panzer Grenadier Division "Reichfuhrer-SS"
17. SS Panzer Grenadier Division "Götz von Berlichingen"
18. SS Freiwilligen Panzer Grenadier Division "Horst Wessel"
19. Waffen Grenadier Division der SS (Lettisches Nr.2)
20. Waffen Grenadier Division der SS (Estnisches Nr.1)
21. Waffen Gebirgs Division der SS "Skanderbeg" (Albanisches Nr.1)
22. Freiwilligen Kavallerie Division der SS "Maria Theresa"
23. Waffen Gebirgs Division der SS "Kama" (Kroatisches Nr. 2)

23. Freiwilligen Panzer-Grenadier Division "Nederland" (from December 1944 after disbandment of "Kama")
24. Waffen Gebirgs Kastjäger Division der SS
25. Waffen Grenadier Division der SS "Hunyadi" (Ungarisches Nr.1)
26. Waffen Grenadier Division der SS (Ungarisches Nr. 2)
27. SS Freiwilligen Grenadier Division "Langemarck"
28. SS Freiwilligen Grenadier Division "Wallonien"
29. Waffen Grenadier Division der SS (Russisches Nr.1)
     This was soon transferred to General Vlassov's Army and the numerical designation was granted to Waffen Grenadier Division der SS (Italienisches Nr. 1) granted to Waffen Grenadier Division der SS (Italienisches Nr.1)
30. Waffen Grenadier Division der SS (Russisches Nr.2)
31. SS Freiwilligen Panzer Grenadier Division "Böhmen-Mähren"
32. SS Panzer Grenadier Division "30 Januar"
33. Waffen Kavallerie Division der SS (Ungarisches Nr.3) (until early 1945)
33. Waffen Grenadier Division "Charlemagne" (Franzosisches Nr.1) (from early 1945).
34. SS Freiwilligen Grenadier Division "Landstorm Nederland"

SS Wachverbände
1., 2., 4., 5., 6., Wach Bataillone
3. Wach Bataillon "Nordwest"
7. Wach Bataillon "Böhmen-Mähren"
8. SS Bataillon Truppenübungsplatz-Debica
9. Wach Bataillon "Nord"
10. Wach Bataillon "Obersalzberg"
11. Wach Bataillon "Orianberg"
12. Wach Bataillon "Prag"
7., 8., 9., 10. Wach Kompagnien
Wach Kompagnie "Hegewald"
Wach Truppen "Böhmen", Heidelager", "Kurmark", Moorlager", "Seelager", "Westpreussen"

Between 1941 and 1945 the following divisions are mentioned in official records but were never actually raised: Gebirgsdivision "Andreas Höfer", SS-Freiwilligen Panzer Grenadier Division "Feldherrnhalle", Finnisches SS Bataillon "Kalevala", SS Division "Niederschsen", SS Division "Reichmarschall", SS Panzer Grenadier Division "Wallenstein" and a Germanisches SS Division "Waräger".

Besides the Officers' Training Academies at Braunschweig and Bad Tölz and the two NCO Training Schools at Lauernberg and Radolfzell the following SS schools had been formed by 1944:
SS Artillerie Schule I "Gau" und II "Beneschau"
SS Junkerschule "Prag"
SS und Waffen Junkerschule Klagenfurt
SS und Waffen Junkerschule Posen Taskau
SS Unterführerschule Arnheim
SS und Waffen Unterführerschule Laibach
SS Unterführerschulen Lublinitz, Posen Taskau und Braunsberg
SS Funktions Unterführerschule Breslau-Lissa
SS Unterführer Schulen Bütow, Eipel, Neustadt am Rudenberg, Rekoe, Wuidau
SS Panzer Grenadier Schule Sophienwalde, Kienschlag, Teinitz

SS Reit und Fahrschule Lingau
SS Kavallerie Schule Damashöhe and Eichenkam
SS Reit und Fahrschule München-Riem
SS Kavallerie Schule Gottingen
SS Reit und Fahrschule Zainose
SS Panzer Schule Binz auf Rügen
SS Panzer schule Celle, Unna
SS Panzerjäger und Sturmgeschütz Schule Beneschau
SS Pionier Schule Hradischko
SS Gebirgschule Stubaital
SS Nachrichten Schule Nurnberg, Stendal, Melnick and Metz-Aussig
SS Kraftfahrschulen I-Spirow, II-Hohenau an der Marsch and III-Schottersberg
SS Kraftfahrschulen Wittersdorf, Dachau and Wien
SS Sanitäts Schulen Wien, Berlin-Lichterfelde, Marburg, Prag Beneschau, und Bad Ausee
SS Spion Abwehr Schule Neustrelitz
SS Dolmetscher Schule Orianberg und Danzig
SS Waffenmeister Schule Dachau
SS Führer Schule der Wirtschafts Verwaltungs-Dienstes Arolsen
SS Musik Schule Braunschweig
SS Reichsschule fur Leibsübungen Prag

Miscellaneous Units

Waffen-Grenadier (SS) Rumanisches Standarte Nr.1
Waffen-Grenadier (SS) Rumanisches Standarte Nr.2
Waffen-Grenadier (SS) Bulgarisches Standarte Nr.1
1. SS Kavallerie Standarte
2. SS Kavallerie Standarte
13. SS Gebirgs Grenadier Standarte "Handschar"
21. SS Gebirgs Grenadier Standarte "Skanderberg"
Franzosischen SS Freiwilligen Sturm Brigade "Charlemagne"
Ski-Bataillon der SS "Norge"
SS Freiwilligen Panzer Grenadier Brigade "Nederland"
Kaukasischer Waffenverbände der SS
Osttürkischer Waffenverbände der SS
Serbisches SS Freiwilligenkorps
Finnisches Freiwilligen Bataillon der Waffen SS
 Schweres Artillerieabteilung 501-505
Nebelwerferabteilung 501-505
Schwere Panzerabteilung 500-503
Panzerjägerabteilung 560
Nachrichtenregimenter 500-503
Wehrgeologenbataillon
Verstärke Totenkopfregimenter 4-14
SS-Jägdverbände 600, 501, 502
SS-Kriegsberichter Standarte — "Kurt Eggers"
SS-Sturm Brigade "RFSS"
SS-Festungsregiment Nr.1, "Besslein"
SS-Fallschirmjäger Bataillone

This listing is by no means complete, but does include all main units and formations. Readers interested in the complete breakdown of all Waffen-SS formations should refer to the definitive works on the subject such as those listed in the introduction.

Comparative Ranks

British	Waffen-SS
General	SS-Oberst-Gruppenführer
Lieut-General	SS-Gruppenführer
Major General	SS-Brigadeführer
Brigadier	SS-Oberführer
Colonel	SS-Standartenführer
Lieut-Colonel	SS-Obersturmbannführer
Major	SS-Sturmbannführer
Captain	SS-Hauptsturmführer
Lieutenant	SS-Obersturmführer
Second Lieutenant	SS-Untersturmführer

Non-commissioned officers cannot be given such precise rank equivalents but the following listing is considered as close as possible.

British	Waffen-SS
Regimental Sergeant Major	SS-Stabsscharführer
Company Sergeant Major	SS-Sturmscharführer
Colour Sergeant/Staff Sgt	SS-Hauptscharführer
Sergeant	SS-Oberscharführer/SS-Standartenjünker
Lance Sergeant	SS-Scharführer
Corporal	SS-Unterscharführer
Lance Corporal	SS-Rottenführer
Private, Trooper, Gunner, Rifleman, etc	SS-Sturmann, SS-Mann later SS-Staffelmann SS-Schütze (there was also an SS-Oberschütze SS-Jäger, SS-Reiter etc)
Untrained recruit	SS-Anwarter

NCOs and other ranks who became officer candidates were distinguished by the wearing of officer quality peaked hats but with black leather chin straps. With this headdress they wore their normal NCO uniform and other ranks' belt. Because this order of dress caused confusion, additional badges of identification were introduced in 1944. These took the form of two strips of 8mm wide grey silk figured NCO collar and shoulder strap lace sewn side by side across the root of the shoulder strap where it was sewn to the jacket at the shoulder seam. The cadets continued to wear the officers' cap. Future NCOs were similarly distinguished. Potential NCOs serving for twelve years had a 9mm wide piece of lace across the shoulder strap by the shoulder seam while the candidate with a potential service of less than twelve years had a 4mm wide twisted cord in his unit waffenfarbe (arm of service colour) across the shoulder straps in the same position.

The Waffen-SS Badges of Rank

The first Political Purpose Troops and the early SS-VT formations wore the same rank badges as the Allgemeine-SS. Up to the rank of SS-Standartenführer these were displayed on the left collar front on a black parallelogram cloth patch. Officers collar patches were black velvet. The ranks of SS-Standartenführer and above were displayed on both collar fronts on black parallelogram cloth patches. The divisional or legion badge was worn on the right collar patch by all junior ranks.

The first collar patches were bordered with a twisted aluminium and black cord for all ranks up to SS-Sturmscharführer and a twisted aluminium cord for all ranks from SS-Untersturmführer and above. Ranks could also be identified by shoulder straps or cords originally worn on the right shoulder only as in the Allgemeine-SS but later on both.

In 1938 the SS-VT were ordered to take Wehrmacht style shoulder straps and sleeve badges into use; thereafter they wore a combination of collar patch, shoulder straps or cords and sleeve badges.

The oak leaves, acorns, stars and bars of the SS badges were derived from the SA (Sturmabteilung) which had in turn used designs which originated in the Freikorps and the Stahlhelm. Oak leaves, etc, of the officers' insignia were silvered aluminium. The aluminium stars of the NCOs were slightly smaller than those used by the officers, and the D figured aluminium (later grey silk) braid which bordered their collars, shoulder straps and sleeve badges was 8mm wide.

In 1940 all Waffen-SS officers of General Officer rank were granted the privilege of equivalent Wehrmacht rank and in the spring of 1942 the rank of SS-Oberstgruppenführer was introduced. This necessitated an alteration in the design of badges for General Officers and an opportunity was taken to modify the design of their badges introducing a more stylish and elongated oak leaf.

NCO's shoulder strap (Unterscharführer) with slip-on "LAH" cypher, shown in more detail at right.

SS—Anwärter
SS—Schütze
SS—Mann
SS—Oberschütze
(with sleeve star)

SS—Sturmann
with one sleeve
chevron.

SS—Rottenführer
with two sleeve chevron.

SS—Unterscharführer

SS—Scharführer

SS—Oberfcharführer

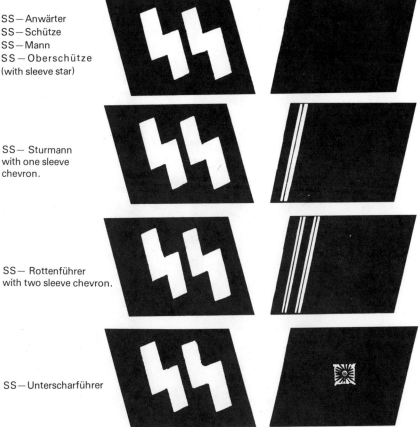

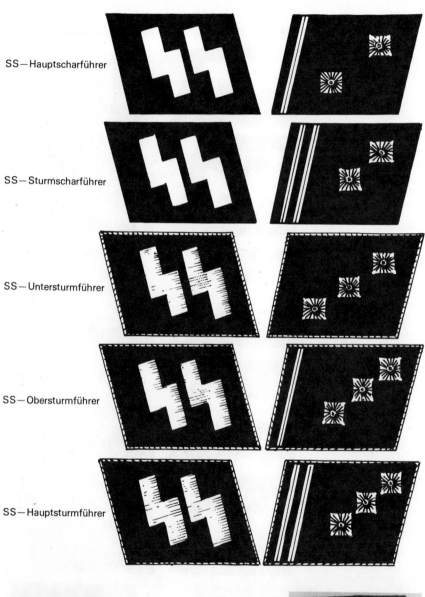

SS—Hauptscharführer

SS—Sturmscharführer

SS—Untersturmführer

SS—Obersturmführer

SS—Hauptsturmführer

Left: SS Sig Runes on a collar patch. Right: Divisional collar patch of Division "Prinz Eugen".

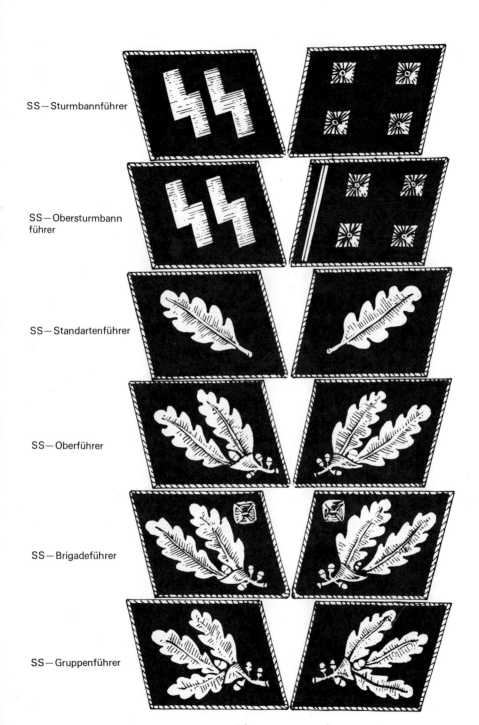

SS—Sturmbannführer

SS—Obersturmbann
führer

SS—Standartenführer

SS—Oberführer

SS—Brigadeführer

SS—Gruppenführer

13

SS—Obergruppenführer

1942-1945

SS—Standartenführer

SS—Oberführer

SS—Brigadeführer

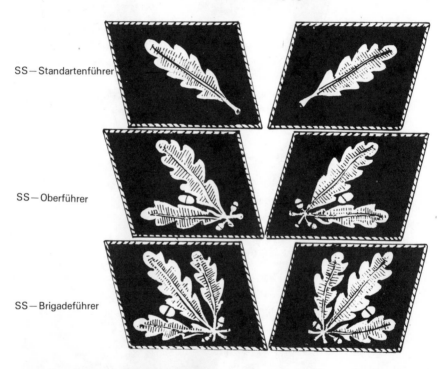

Left: Divisional collar patch and collar lace of an NCO of a "Totenkopfs" Standarte. Opposite page: collar patch detail of a SS-Gruppenführer (Generalleutant der Waffen-SS), in 1943.

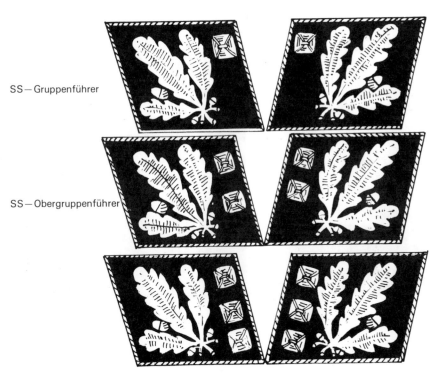

SS—Gruppenführer

SS—Obergruppenführer

SS—Oberst-Gruppenführer

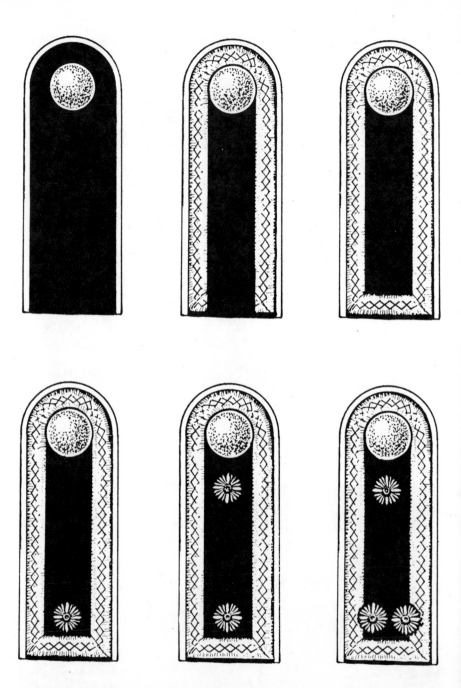

Left to right, top to bottom. SS-Sturmmann/SS-Schütze, SS-Unterscharführer. SS-Scharführer, Oberscharführer, Hauptscharführer, Sturmscharführer.

16

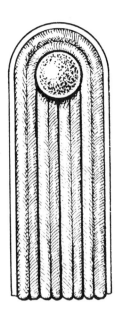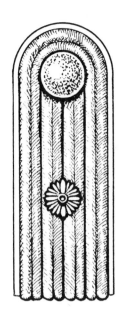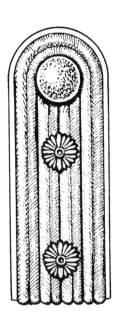

Left to right: Untersturmführer, Obersturmführer, Hauptsturmführer.

Left: SS-Schütze, showing collar patches, shoulder straps, first pattern SS field grey blouse (1939 issue) with open collar, worn with tie and (in this case) a civilian shirt which was authorised due to clothing shortages. Note "Schiffchen" forage cap.

17

Left to right, top to bottom: Sturmbannführer, Obersturmbannführer, Standarten-
führer, Oberführer; Brigadeführer, Gruppenführer, Obergruppenführer,
Oberstgruppenführer.

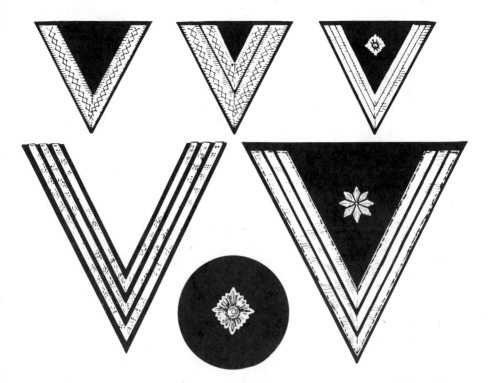

Top row, left to right: SS-Sturmmann, SS-Rottenführer (both worn on left arm); chevron worn by former Wehrmacht and Ordnungspolizei personnel. The star was worn by men who had served in the Wehrmacht or Ordnungspolizei while already members of the SS. This distinction was introduced in July 1935 (worn on right arm). Bottom row, left to right: chevron worn by personnel who were SS or NSDAP members before 1933. This insignia was also worn by former members of the Wehrmacht and Ordnungspolizei until July 1935 (worn on right arm). Oberschutze a star (worn on left arm). Enlarged detail of star shown in top row right.

Shoulder Strap Devices

Regiments of the SS-VT wore Gothic cyphers on their shoulder straps:

"Leibstandarte"	— LAH	"Germania"	— G
"Deutschland"	— D	"Der Führer"	— DF

These were grey embroidered for the NCOs and troopers and in bronze or aluminium for the officers. Similarly the staff of the two Officers Academies carried cyphers:

Bad Tölz	JS	Braunschweig	JS
	T		B

Medical commissioned staff wore an Aescapalian Staff on the shoulder cords. SS-Totenkopfverbände and SS-Totenkopfregimenten wore numerals beneath the deathshead on their collar patch and in some cases numerals on their shoulder straps also.

Examples of shoulder strap insignia, left to right, top to bottom: Sturmscharführer of Junkerschule Bad Tölz; SS-Unterscharführer (SS-Junker); SS-Schütze of SS-VT Regiment "Der Führer"; SS-Schütze of "SS Leibstandarte Adolf Hitler"; SS-Schütze (SS-Unterführeranwarter) of SS-VT Regiment "Deutschland"; SS-Schütze (Unterführeranwarter) SS-VT Regiment "Germania".

Arm of Service Colours — Waffenfarbe

Towards the end of 1939 the SS-VT were ordered to wear the arm of service colours used by the Army on their new style shoulder straps, and on their field service caps. The piping on the officers' peaked caps and on their long trousers were to remain white as before. However many of the officers began to use coloured piping on these garments also and in the early summer of 1940 this unauthorised practice was partially recognised when Himmler gave permission for the waffenfarbe to be worn on their peaked caps. Later the same year this order was rescinded and officers were reminded quite strongly that they must revert to white again. Nevertheless it appears this order was ignored by many units. NCOs and other ranks wore the bright coloured pipings on their field service caps and on the shoulder straps, and in Panzer-Division "Wiking" 5. Panzer Regiment had the added distinction of pink piping around their collar patches.

Waffenfarbe colours

Arm	Colour	German
Reichfuhrer's personal staff	Dark Grey	Dunkelgrau
General Officers	Light Grey	Hellgrau
SS Main Office staff	Light Grey	Hellgrau
Divisional staffs	White	Weiss
Artillery units & schools	Bright Red	Hochrot
Engineer & pioneer units & schools	Black	Schwarz
Cavalry units and schools	Golden yellow	Goldgelb
Infantry units & schools	White	Weiss
Transportation troops	Light Pink	Hellrosa
Armoured units	Pink	Rosa
Signal units and schools	Lemon Yellow	Zitrongelb
Reconnaissance units	Copper brown	Kupferbraun
Supply units	Light Blue	Hellblau
Medical units	Cornflower Blue	Kornblumenblau
Veterinary staff	Crimson Red	Karmesinrot
Alpine rifle units	Grass Green	Wiesengrün
Special services	Orange Red	Orangerot
Specialist staff	Red and grey twist	Rotgrau
Judge Advocate staff	Wine Red	Bordeauxrot
Field police	Orange	Orange
War correspondents	Lemon Yellow	Zitrongelb
Totenkopfstandarten	White	Zeiss
Anti-tank units	Pink	Rosa
Rocket troops	Wine Red	Bordeauxrot
Tank engineers	Black and white twist	Schwarzweiss
Officers on the reserve	Dark Green	Dunkelgrün

SS-VT and Waffen-SS unit collar patches

The early SS-VT formations all wore the SS-runes on the right collar patch although many regiments and other formations added either numerals, an initial letter, or symbols. The LAH wore the runes only but regiments "Deutschland", "Germania" and "Der Fuhrer" added the Arabic numeral 1, 2 or 3. Besides its distinctive cuff title the SS-Nachrichtensturmbann added a streak of lightning after the runes and the SS-Pioniersturmbann added crossed pickaxes and shovels. The SS-Verwaltungschule added a Gothic 'V' and the officers' training schools similarly added either a Gothic or Roman 'T' for Bad Tölz and 'B' for Braunschweig. The SS-Sanitätsabteilung wore a Gothic 'S' after their runic SS.

As the Waffen-SS grew in size and stature during the early years of the war it became the rule that the true Germanic formations wore the SS-runes and the foreign legions and later divisions wore formation patch badges which were easily identifiable as having particular national characteristics. The Odal rune of the "Prinz Eugen" division, and the Arm and Scimitar of "Handschar" are both examples of this. However true German personnel serving with these divisions, either as part of the staff or on detachment, continued to wear their SS-rune badges, and indeed in some formations some of the foreign personnel also appear to have worn the Germanic runes instead of their divisional badge. Several formation badges were ordered to be manufactured or considered but were never issued. In some cases they may have had a limited distribution but no photographic evidence remains.

Two divisions departed from these rules. One was 4. Polizei Panzer-Grenadier Division who were initially permitted to wear their police tunics and two grey embroidered laces on a bright green Waffenfarbe on both collar fronts. Later they were issued with army style field blouses with SS-rune formation patches. The second unit which must be specially mentioned is 3. SS Panzer Division "Totenkopf". Originating in the Totenkopf Regiment formations they wore the Deathshead as a formation badge. The skull was worn in various ways by all ranks and in some cases on both collar patches. Later in the war some members of the division wore the SS-runes.

In the "Wiking" division some unit commanders wore the runic badge on both collar patches and the same practice with two Odal runes was adopted in the "Prinz Eugen" Division. In these cases the officers' rank was distinguished by the shoulder cords only. Artur Phleps divisional commander of the Prinz Eugen Division wore his Odal runes on a diamond shaped patch on the left sleeve.

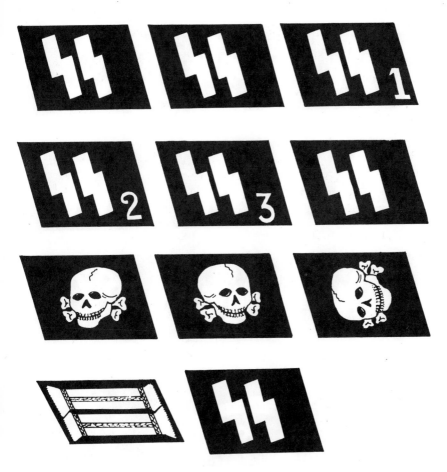

Early divisional and regimental collar patches: Left to right, top to bottom: 1st Div (LAH); 2nd Div. ("Das Reich"); Standarte "Deutschland"; Standarte "Germania"; Standarte "Der Führer"; 3rd. Div. ("Totenkopf") variant; 3rd. Div. ("Totenkopf") Deathshead worn on some right collar patches; 3rd. Div. variant; 3rd Div. variant; 4th Div. ("Polizei") police insignia; 4th. Div. SS insignia.

Cuff title of "Leibstandarte Adolf Hitler" and, later, the LAH division.

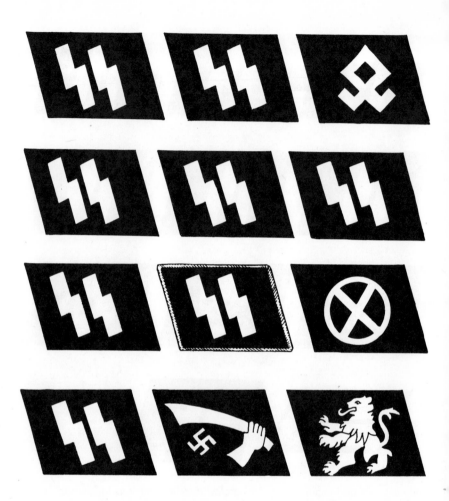

Regimental or divisional collar patches. Left to right, top to bottom: 5th (Wiking), 6th (Nord), 7th (Prinz Eugen); 8th (Florian Geyer), 9th (Hohenstaufen), 10th (Frundsberg); 11th (Nordland), 11th (H v S). 11th (variation); 12th (Hitler Jugend), 13th (Handschar), 14th (Galizische Nr. 1).

Cuff title of 10.SS-Div. "Frundsberg".

Frundsberg

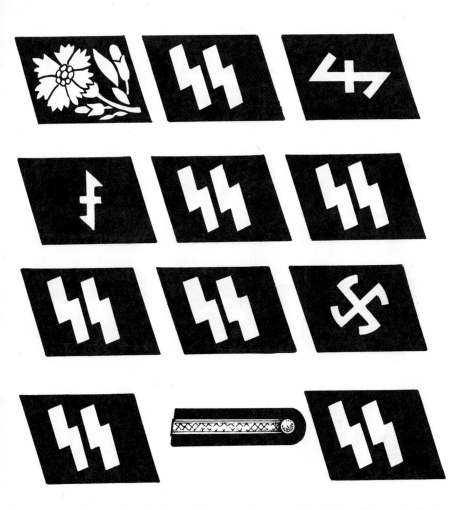

Divisional collar patches. Left to right, top to bottom: 22nd (Maria Theresa); 23rd (Kama and Nederland), 23rd (Nederland); 23rd (Nederland, variation), 24th, 25th; 26th, 27th, 27th (variation); 28th, 29th (Russisches Nr.1 — worn on both collar fronts, 29th (Italisches Nr1).

Cuff title of Freiwilligen Legion "Nederland".

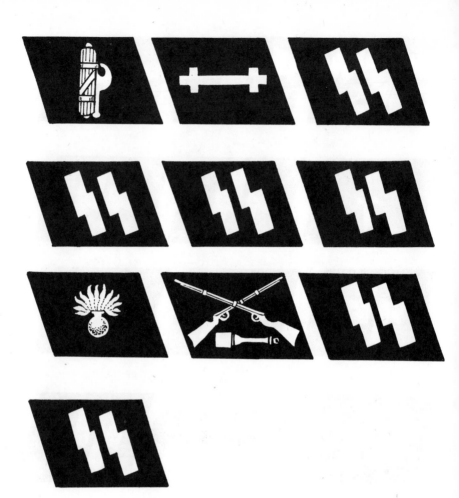

Divisional collar patches. Left to right, top to bottom: 29th (Italienische Nr.1), 30th (Russiches Nr.2), 31st; 32nd (30 Januar), 33rd (Ungarische Nr.3), 34th (Landstorm Nederland); 34th variant, 36th (Dirlewanger), 37th (Lutzow); 38th (Nibelungen).

Cuff title of 33. Waffen Gren. Div. "Charlemagne", a 1945 formation of French volunteers.

Divisional collar patches. Left to right, top to bottom: 15th (Lettisches Nr.1) 16th (Reichsführer-SS), 17th; 18th (Horst Wessel), 19th (Lettisches Nr.2), 19th (variation); 20th (Estnisches Nr.1), 20th (variation), 20th (variation); 20th (variation), 21st (Albanisches Nr.1), 21st (variation).

Cuff title of 16.SS Pz. Gren. Div. "Reichsführer-SS".

Reichsführer-᛬᛬

Divisional collar patches either produced but not issued, or alleged to have been issued, but for which no photographic evidence has been traced. Left to right, top to bottom: 5th (Viking), 23rd (Kama), 24th, 25 (Hunyadi-Ungerisches Nr.2), 27th (Langemarck), 29th (Russisches Nr.1); 30th (Russisches Nr.2), 30th (variation), 30th (variation); 33rd (Ungarisches Nr.3), 33rd (Charlemagne — originally to be Jeanne d'Arc); 15th (Lettisches Nr.1), Unidentified — believed to be trial pattern for 36th (Dirlewanger).

Foreign Units

Foreign personnel serving with the Waffen-SS were identified by a coloured, machine embroidered arm badge in a pattern which made their country of origin easily recognisable.

In general the SS national arm badges were simple shields with flat tops and curved sides, although exceptions are known. In some cases several patterns of arm badge appear to have been worn by the same unit at the same time.

Until 1944 these shields were worn 1.5cm above the cuff title on the left sleeve of the field blouse, but from that year they were ordered to be worn 1.5cm below the sleeve eagle and above any sleeve chevron or star. It goes without saying that these regulations were not always obeyed. Indeed variations in the position of the badges appear within the same formation at the same period and in some cases were abandoned altogether in favour of small cloth representations of the individual's national flag.

Photographs reveal that, in some cases, Wehrmacht pattern national arm badges were worn by SS troops and on the right sleeve. This could have occurred when a recent transfer from army to SS had occurred.

Freikorps Danmark
Collar patch: At first this unit, as the Schalburg Korps, wore the SS Sun Wheel. Later the SS runes were worn.
Armshield: Firstly a yellow shield with three bright blue crowned lions passant and red hearts. Later a red shield with a white cross or a red pennon with a white cross.
Cuff title: "Freikorps Danmark" or "Danmark".

Legion Flandern
Collar patch: The swastika with the curved arms or the SS runes.
Arm shield: A dull yellow shield with a black rampant lion with a knotted or a single tail.
Cuff title: "Legion Flandern".

Legion Wallonie
Collar patch: The SS runes. An unconfirmed report that the Ragged Cross of Burgundy was produced.
Arm shield: Vertical black, yellow and red bands. A black panel across the top of the shield lettered in yellow upper case letters "Wallonie"
Cuff title: "Wallonie" or "Wallonien".

Legion Niederlande
Collar patch: The Wolfangel rune either vertically or horizontally.
Armshield: Orange, white and blue diagonals (either right or left) or horizontal bars. An oblong flag of horizontal orange white and blue also worn.
Cuff title: "Frw. Legion Nederland".

An orange white and blue decal was worn on the left side of the helmet for ceremonial occasions.

Legion Norwegen
Collar patch: White rampant lion carrying an axe.
Arm shield: A shield or a flag in the Norwegian national flag design. An arm badge comprising the lion carrying the axe also alleged to have been worn.
Cuff title: "Frw. Legion Norwegen".

Veterans of the Norwegian "Hird" were permitted to wear their emblem on their Waffen-SS tunics. This was a red circlet with a silver grey cross and two swords. The badge was worn above the cuff title on the left arm.

Finnisches Freiwilligen Battalion
Collar patch: SS-runes
Arm shield: Black, white edged, rectangular shield with a white Finnish crowned lion with mailed front leg carrying a sword over it's shoulder and standing on a curved Russian sword.
Cuff title: "Finnisches FRW. Bataillon der Waffen-SS".

Estnisches Legion
Collar patch: SS-runes or the double swastika.
Arm shield: Shield with horizontal bands of pale blue, black and white. Alternative a shield with diagonal stripes and three lions passant or three black lions on a yellow shield.
Cuff title: None.

Lettisches Legion
Collar patch: SS-runes or a Swastika.
Arm shield: Several versions known. Basically a red shield with a white diagonal with or without "LATVIJA" on a black or red panel above or in the top left corner.
Cuff title: None.

Franzosisches Freiwillen Legion der Waffen SS
Collar patch: SS-runes or the "Flaming Sword" which is alleged to have been the original design for the "Charlemagne" Division.
Arm shield: Shield with the French tricolour blue white and red vertical stripe.
Cuff title: Alleged to have been "Charlemagne".

Britisches Freikorps
Collar patch: Three lions or leopards passant guardant.
Arm shield: The Union Jack.
Cuff title: "Britisches Freikorps".

Alleged to have worn British uniforms with German badges. In January 1945 the British Army occupied Spiedelberg Kaserne at Lengo. British personnel cleaning out the attic of the barrack block in 1945 found a number of uniforms, some leather equipment, miscellaneous daily orders, etc. One of the uniforms had a Union Jack arm shield on the left sleeve. It had the Wehrmacht National Emblem on the right breast and army style collar badges.

Italienisches Freiwilligen Legion der Waffen SS
Collar patch: The SS-runes or the Roman "fasces".
Arm shield: Black with yellow threadwork edging and the "fasces" in yellow picked out with red, or shield in national colours on a black backing.
Cuff title: None.
Sleeve eagle: Special design clutching "fasces" in its talons in grey, on red cloth.

At first the Legion (later the Freiwilligen Sturmbrigade "Italien") had red collar patches with rank badges on both and wore Italian camouflaged clothing and Italian caps and helmets.

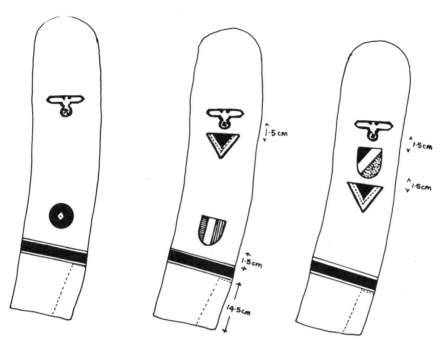

Regulation positions for arm badges, arm shields, and cuff titles.

Foreign Legion collar patches. Left to right, top to bottom: Denmark, Flanders, Norway; Netherlands, Netherland (variation), Finnish Volunteers; Legion of St. George, India, East Turkish Volunteers.

31

Serbisches Freiwillen Korps
Collar patch: Plain black.
Arm shield and cuff title not known.

Östturkischer Waffen-Verband der SS
Collar patch: SS-runes or Turkish sword diagonally under a round shield.
Arm shield: Not known.
Cuff title: "Östturkischer Waffen-Verband der SS".

Indisches Legion
Collar patch: Plain black.
Arm shield: Army type dull yellow white and green horizontal bands with a leaping tiger. Unit wore turbans.
Cuff title: None.

The SS Emblem
The principal SS emblem was the Totenkopf (Deathshead), a skull with bones. This badge, which was a symbol used by military daredevil units since the period of Gustav Adolphus and adopted subsequently by French revolutionary units, regiments of Frederick the Great's Prussian Army, Spanish guerrillas and British units, was worn by all ranks on the head dress, on some unit collar patches, on cuff titles, drum shells, trumpet banners, flags and vehicles. It was either aluminium, silver-plated, embroidered in white or grey silk or cotton, or painted white on a black ground.

The second SS emblem was a special form of the Hoheitsabzeichen (national emblem) — the Eagle — heraldically designed with its head to the left and wings outstretched and clutching, in its talons a circlet, of oakleaves or laurel bound with ribbons in which the ubiquitous swastika was set. A small version of the SS version of this emblem appeared on the head dress, either in metal or in white or grey embroidery on grey or black grounds. From 1936 a distinctive version of the emblem was worn on the left sleeve of the tunic, blouses and greatcoat. The badge was initially in grey or white silk on a black backing but from 1938 most of the officers appear to have adopted aluminium sleeve eagles while the NCOs and men wore similar shaped eagles in white or grey silk.

Some officers seem to have worn the Wehrmacht type breast eagle on their sleeves and the badge continued to be worn on much of the camouflage (except the smock) clothing in flagrant disregard of orders concerning the wearing of badges on clothing without shoulder straps (see under Camouflaged Clothing).

Opposite: Examples of SS VT and Waffen SS Flags and Standards
The large flag at the top of page illustrates an example of a battalion flag of an SS-VT Regiment. Note the small black rectangle in the upper corner which indicates the Regiment and the battalion, in this case the second battalion of Regiment "Germania". The standard on the right, top of page, is a typical example of an SS Standard, in this case the standard of the "Leibstandarte". Note the title of the regiment in the black box beneath the National Emblem. The left hand example in the next row is the Standard of an SS "Totenkopf" Regiment. Note the Deathshead in the centre of the black box with a Roman numeral indicating the identity of the regiment at either end. An enlarged example of the design of a typical Deathshead is given in the centre. On the right of this row is the later pattern Standard carried by the "Leibstandarte". Note the gold wreath, the four gold National Emblems and the gold border and cords with tassels which were the same as the Führer's personal Standard. The two lower flags are examples of the type of battalion, squadron, or battery flags carried by the Waffen-SS during the war. The example on the left is an infantry battalion flag, while the right hand swallow tailed flag is a cavalry pattern. Note that the ground of these flags was in waffenfarbe colour.

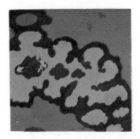 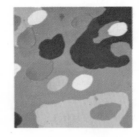 

 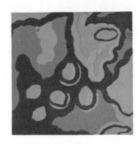 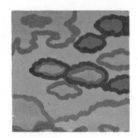

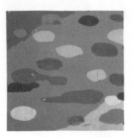 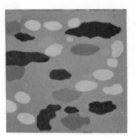

The patterns for camouflage clothing, reproduced from actual garments in the Imperial War Museum, London. Approximately half full-size.

Autumn (Fall)	Spring	Summer
Summer	Autumn (Fall)	Summer
	Autumn (Fall)	Spring

Read from left to right, top to bottom. Note the alternative patterns for each season.

The Rune Breast Badge

Full ethnic German members of the SS serving with police units wearing police badges or with foreign divisions where the unit collar patch was not the Sig-runes wore a diamond shaped patch of grey-green cloth beneath the left breast pocket of the field blouse embroidered with the SS runes.

Aiguillettes

In some units Waffen SS officers wore an aluminium wire aiguillette as a badge to indicate they were on duty. Adjutants similarly wore an aiguillette of a special type to signify their appointment. Orderly NCOs wore an aluminium cord aiguillette looped around the right shoulder as a badge of their duty.

Gorgets

Three types were worn. By the Feldgendarmerie; by standard bearers and by unit Provost patrols "Striefendienst".

Above, left: Special SS pattern aiguillette worn by adjutants for parades and ceremonial. Right: Wehrmacht pattern aluminium cord aiguillette worn by Waffen-SS officers for parade dress and special occasions. Below: Feldgendarmerie duty gorget (ringkragen) — eagle and lettering in luminous paint, and standard bearer's gorget — polished steel with gold coloured devices

33

Head dress

The original head dress of the Political-Purpose units and the SS-VT was the peaked cap which was also worn by the Algemeine-SS. The cap was black with white pipings. Officers wore caps with velvet cap bands and aluminium twisted cords which also had white pipings. NCOs and other ranks had black leather chin straps. The cap for all ranks had a black leather or artificial fibre peak and a small silver coloured aluminium button on either side.

The first undress field cap worn by the Bereitschaften was a round black peakless head dress similar to the mütze of the old German Army. It had white pipings and a white metal button with a Deathshead device beneath a small national emblem worn on the front of the cap. NCOs wore a similar undress cap but with a small black peak and a black leather chin strap.

However, a grey undress field cap was issued shortly after and was worn with the first grey uniform. This cap was the first of the schiffchen (ship) shape which later became the almost universal field service cap of the German Army until the introduction of the peaked Einheitsmütze. The 'ship' cap had a large white metal button on the front embossed with a Deathshead and had a white national emblem (Hoheitsabzeichen), eagle and swastika on a black triangular background sewn on the left side. Later the large metal button was discarded in favour of a large grey embroidered or white metal Deathshead.

In 1939 the Waffen-SS adopted the Army style of inverted chevron of Waffenfarbe piping (called the soutache) which was worn on the front of the cap, enclosing first the metal button and later the Deathshead. In 1942 this chevron of brightly coloured cloth was ordered to be discontinued but photographs reveal that it was still being worn by some units until late in the war.

NCOs were permitted to wear field grey service caps with black cap bands and grey cloth peaks. These caps had the stiffening wire of the upper part removed so that they could be easily folded and tucked under shoulder straps or put in the pocket. They had either grey embroidered or white metal Deathshead and national emblem badges on the front. The 'ship' cap was also worn by NCOs.

After the introduction of the field grey clothing Waffen-SS officers wore grey caps with black velvet bands and white piping and aluminium cords. See under Waffenfarbe (page 21) for reference to coloured pipings on this cap. Some troopers bought as personal items grey peaked caps with black bands and white pipings and black leather chin straps for walking out.

The first pattern officers' quality 'ship'-shaped cap was introduced in 1940. This cap had a bright aluminium piping around the deep turn-up and it had the SS national emblem and the Deathshead on the front, either in white metal, or in aluminium embroidery on black cloth backing. Black versions of the 'ship'-shaped cap were provided for armoured and reconnaissance units wearing the special black blothing and a version of the original field cap was also provided in black to be worn with the pre-war black service tunic and breeches.

A brown-green tropical helmet was worn by troops wearing tropical clothing in Southern Russia, Greece and other Balkan stations. Detachable metal shields were worn on this head dress with SS-runes and the swastika badge as worn on the SS steel helmet. The helmet had a brown leather chin strap.

Early in the war a large black cloth beret fitted over a close fitting crash helmet was worn by armoured and reconnaissance units. This cap was decorated with large grey

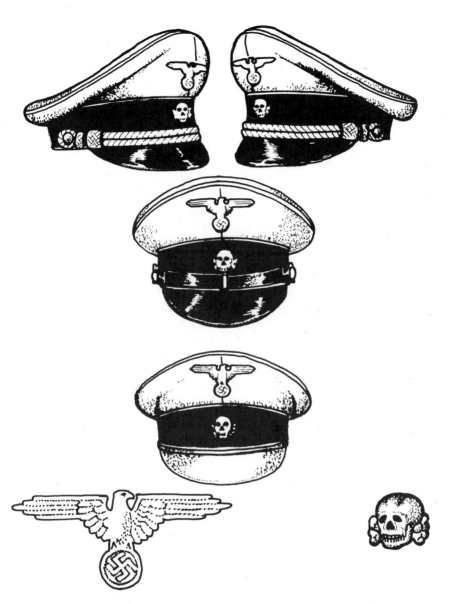

General officers cap (aluminium piping)

Field officers cap (white
piping and stitched peak binding)

NCO's and other ranks cap
NCO's field cap, cloth peak

National emblem

Deathshead

Members of 13. "Handschar" Division wearing the red Bosnian fez. Note also the divisional collar patches.
caption 8

embroidered national emblem and Deathshead badges.

In 1943 a new pattern field service cap with a large flat cloth peak based on the mountain troops cap and known as the Einheitsmütze was introduced for all ranks of the Waffen-SS on active service. A tropical version of this cap was also issued. The field grey version had a deep flap which could be unhooked and folded down over the ears and was fastened in front by one or two buttons. The normal national emblem and Deathshead badges appeared on this cap either separately, or with the eagle badge worn on the side. Some caps had both eagle and Deathshead badges applied to the cap sewn on one piece of grey cloth. Officers' versions of the cap had the aluminium cording around the top seam of the crown. Mountain Divisions wore the Waffen-SS version of the Edelweiss badge on a black backing on the left side. The tropical version of the Einheitmütze had no flap and was worn without buttons on the front. Its badges were yellow coloured silk on a black ground. The camouflaged versions of the cap were lightweight, and had no flap and no buttons on the front. However photographs show that some officers provided themselves with camouflaged caps with the flap and in some cases with buttons on the front and with badges.

Personnel of the Moslem Divisions, "Handschar" and "Kama" wore the Bosnian fez. Several patterns are known to have been worn; a low field grey version with a rounded top and a long black or bottle green tassel; a taller more conventional fez in field grey with a green tassel on a long cord; a dark red fez with a dark bottle green cord and tassel. Green fez's are also known to be worn. A lower round-topped red cap is also said to have been worn. In one photograph personnel seem to be wearing a light grey conical cap. All Moslem head dress were worn with the national emblem and the Deathshead badge.

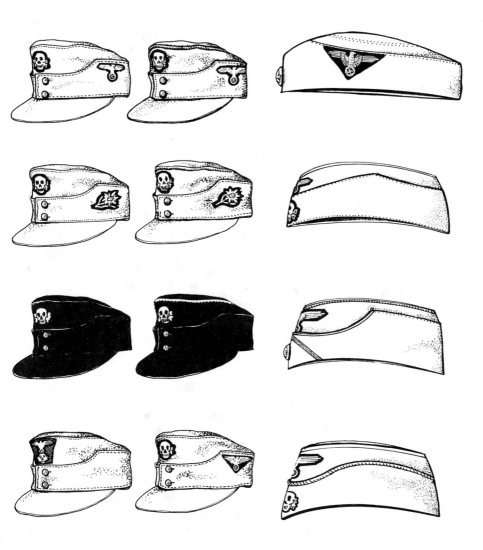

Einheitsmütze		Schiffchen Feldmütze
Other ranks, 1943-44	Officers, 1943-44	SS-VT original type
SS-Mountain Troops other ranks	SS-Mountain Troops officers	SS-VT later type
SS-Panzer Troops other ranks	SS-Panzer Troops officers	1939 Army pattern
Other ranks 1944-45 (printed badges)	Officers 1944-45 (printed badges)	Officers pattern 1939 on

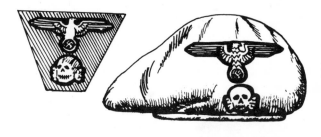

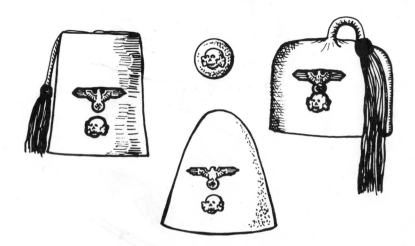

Camouflaged Einheitsmütze (two versions)

SS-Panzer Troops black tank headwear (and versions of printed cloth insignia)

Three versions of Bosnian fez (and Deathshead button)

Top: Men of a SS artillery unit wearing the 1937 pattern field service cap and Army pattern field grey service dress, 1940. Above: SS soldiers in Jugoslavia. December 1943, showing the 1940 pattern field service cap (on left) and the einheitsmütze forage cap.

The Steel Helmet

When they were first formed the armed units of the SS wore the ungainly M1916 pattern steel helmet with its deep eye and neck guard and ugly ventilators. The helmet was originally painted black but some units used helmets painted matt grey. Devices painted on this early issue helmet varied. In some cases the Army type of red white and black shield was worn. In other examples a black swastika edged in white was worn on the right side often on a black diamond. Other helmets had the national red white and black shield on the left side and a silver black edged shield with black SS runes on the right.

Subsequently a black shield with white SS runes was used but the final helmet escutcheons were brought into use for the smaller and simple M1935 helmet which consisted of a white, black edged shield on the right side with black SS runes and a red shield with a white circlet in its centre bearing the black swastika on the left side. First issues of the 1935 helmet were also painted black but were soon issued in matt grey to correspond with the field grey field service uniforms. Later in the war orders were issued for the discontinuance of the painted devices on the helmet but they continued to be worn by most SS troops until the end of the war. Photographs show some Waffen-SS wearing helmets with the runic badge on the left side.

Members of the 4. SS-Polizei Panzer-Grenadier Division wore the wreathed police eagle on the left side and the red shield with the white circlet and the swastika on the right. Later in the war they took the SS-rune badge into use. The police eagle badge comprised a silvered eagle surrounded by a silvered wreath on a black shield edged with a silver line.

A shaped helmet cover, made of the same fabric as the camouflage smock, was issued when the smock was taken into use. The cover came in the same range of colour patterns as the smocks. Dull metal clips and lacing held the cover tight over the helmet. Some covers had loops sewn in to take camouflage garnish. A fringe type face mask in green or field grey material was issued to certain infantry troops; it attached to the helmet in the manner shown opposite. It could be seen worn with the fringe part thrown back over the helmet crown when not required to mask the face.

The 1935 pattern steel helmet (stalhelm).

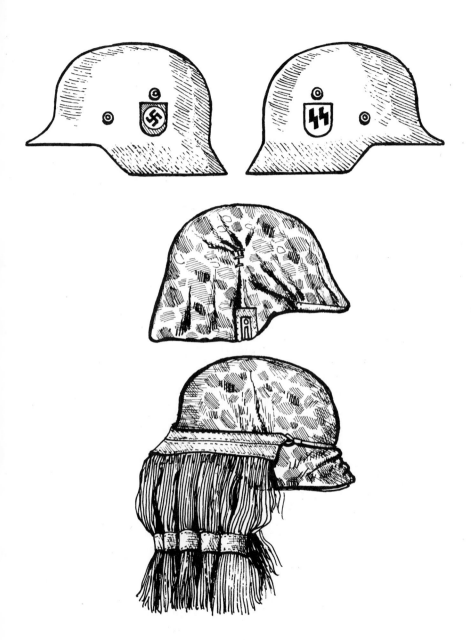

M1935 pattern helmet, left and right sides, with insignia

Helmet cover attached

Fringe-type face mask attached to helmet

41

Tunics and Field Blouses

The first SS-VT units wore the black service tunic as also worn by the Allgemeine-SS. Black breeches and knee-length boots and the black, white piped peak cap completed the Uniform. The tunic was a single-breasted coat with four aluminium buttons down the front and two at the rear at waist level on either side of a central vent. The tunic had two breast patch pockets with scalloped flaps and pleats and two slashed pockets set on the slant in the sides of the skirts with scalloped flaps also fastened with aluminium buttons. The coat had deep turned back cuffs and the collar was edged with twisted aluminium and black cording, all aluminium for the officers. NCOs and other ranks wore it with a brown shirt and black tie. Some officers also wore brown shirts but others wore white collars with this tunic. The red brassard (with white circle, black swastika and with a black stripe near either edge) was worn on the left upper sleeve.

In 1935 a grey tunic (called 'earth-grey') was issued to SS-VT units. It was identical in cut to the black service uniform coat and was worn by all ranks although the officers usually had theirs tailored privately. The tunic of the NCOs and other ranks still had the four button front although it was made so that it could be closed across the chest at the neck with the collar folded down. Officers still retained the four button style and wore it with a white collar and black tie. The brassard was worn with the grey tunic at first but later a sleeve eagle badge replaced it.

At first the simple Allgemeine-SS twisted shoulder cords were worn with this coat. These were black with aluminium twist or plain aluminium according to rank and were worn initially on the right shoulder only and later on both shoulders, but later NCOs and other ranks began to wear a point ended form of the Wehrmacht shoulder strap, edged with black and aluminium cord.

In 1937 a field-grey blouse was designed and introduced for the SS-VT. This garment was single-breasted with four buttons down the front. The front could be closed across the chest and kept fastened by a small point-ended tab, which was stitched to the underside of the right collar front, and by a small horn button. The coat had two patch pockets with scalloped flaps on the breasts but retained the slanting SS type slash pockets in the sides of the skirts. The rear of the coat had a simple central vent, which did not reach to the waist, and plain cuffs with small fly covered buttons on the back seams. The collar was grey and was worn with or without the unit and rank collar patches. The patches and the collar were edged with twisted black and aluminium cording. The twisted cord on the patches seems to have been short lived but the corded edge to collar was still in use on many of the coats as late as 1940.

By the early spring of 1940 Army type field blouses began to be issued to the Waffen-SS (Armed-SS). At first this blouse had a dark green collar and unless the man was in the field or on exercises the collar was worn open and with a brown shirt and black tie. Later a grey shirt was used. The coat had five buttons down the single-breasted front and four large patch pockets the two lower ones reaching almost to the bottom edge. Each pocket had a scalloped flap and wide pleats. Shortly after its

---

Opposite: Tunic patterns. (Top left) Black service tunic. (Top right) Earth grey field blouse. (Bottom left) Earth grey field blouse with extra buttons and fittings for Army style shoulder straps. (Bottom right) SS officers white summer tunic.

introduction the collar was made plain grey and began to be worn closed. Later versions of the coat had simpler oblong pocket flaps. The expensive pocket pleats were also discarded. The field blouse had a shallow vent at the rear and was fitted with special hooks to support the belts. The old point-ended black shoulder straps had also been discarded early in the war and from then the Waffen-SS almost universally used Army style round ended shoulder straps and their own sleeve badges (see page 10).

In 1944 a simplified blouse, waist length and influenced by the British battledress blouse, began to appear. Known as the Feldbluse (Field Blouse) M1944 it was issued primarily to the Army and most photographs of the Waffen-SS in the later stages of the war shown them still wearing the field blouse of the earlier pattern. The coat had six buttons down the single breasted front, the lower two on the close fitting part. There were also two buttons placed horizontally on the lower rear of the blouse. The neck of this blouse was almost always worn open by the rank and file and without a tie. Officers wore it with a collar and tie. The blouse had two simple breast pockets without pleats and with oblong flaps.

Officers, NCOs and men of the armoured and reconnaissance units wore special black clothing said to have been designed to save oil stains showing, but it was liked by the men who were issued with it and they wore it on every possible occasion even when walking out and on leave. The black field jacket of this clothing was a short, waist-length coat, fastened with seven black buttons. The coat front was made to close vertically down the front and had a deep fly to cover the buttons. It could be worn closed at the neck but was more usually worn open with collar and tie. The collar of the officers' coats were usually piped with aluminium cord or, for SS Panzer Regiment Nr.5 "Hermann von Salza" of the Wiking Division, with bright pink waffenfarbe although this distinction is contested by some authorities. It may be that the bright pink cording was worn by officers NCOs and men of other regiments also. NCOs of the armoured units and reconnaissance units did not wear 8mm NCO lace on their collars. The black armoured and reconnaissance unit jacket was worn with specially designed tapered black trousers with slanting pockets on the front of the thighs and buttoning at the ankle. In 1941 a field grey version of this jacket was produced for self-propelled gun units with grey versions of the special trousers, and in 1942 the use of this grey jacket and trousers was extended to self propelled anti-tank gun units.

The original SS-VT drill and fatigue uniform jacket was a light stone or 'cememt-grey' colour twill and was made in the same style as the field blouse. During the early part of the war this was replaced by 'rush green' drill clothing. The rush green drill uniform coat resembled the army patten field blouse in cut but had two patch pockets in the skirts only, a very low folded down collar without unit or rank patches, and had no shoulder straps. However some versions were issued which differed from the original pattern in having collar patches, shoulder straps and breast pockets. Subsequently rush green versions of the armoured/self propelled gun jacket and trousers were issued.

Later in the war a lightweight camouflaged drill and field uniform was introduced. This clothing was made of drill and had a camouflaged pattern on one side and was plain rush green on the other. It had no shoulder straps and collar patches were not worn, consequently the special badges for this type of clothing were worn on the left sleeve.

Opposite: Tunic patterns. (Top left) Army pattern field blouse in common use from 1940 on. (Top right) Field blouse, 1944 pattern. (Bottom left) Special AFV clothing. (Bottom right) White linen summer tunic for NCOs and men.

Officers wore white summer tunics during the first years of war. These had eight aluminium buttons down the front and had breast and skirts patch pockets with scalloped flaps and pleats. The rear of the jackets were finished with a vent to the waist and two hip level buttons. The coat was worn with collar patches, shoulder cords and sleeve eagle, cuff title and national badges where applicable.

In certain units, such as the "Leibstandandarte" white tunics were also worn by NCOs and men during the summer. These had four buttons down the front and had very short skirts with no vent in the rear but a yoked back. The officers' white jackets also had the yoked back. The white jackets for NCOs and other ranks were also worn by mess waiters and other staff. Films of Berschtesgarten show Waffen-SS mess personnel wearing this coat with collar patches, shoulder straps and cuff titles.

Waffen-SS troops also wore tropical uniform in several theatres. The tunic was a cotton twill sand brown and was cut in the style of the standard Wehrmacht tunic as worn by the Afrika Korps. It was normally worn open at the neck with a tie and shirt. In combat conditions a tie or shirt might well be discarded. The sleeve eagle was a special pattern in yellow silk on a black background. This coat was worn by some SS troops in Southern Russia, Greece, Rumania and Italy. It was normally worn with either the loose Afrika Korps style full trousers gathered at the ankle or breeches with brown boots and laced gaiters. Both the sun helmet and sand-brown einheitsmütze were worn with this uniform. Officers often wore custom made tunics of superior quality cloth and some even continued to wear the old SS-VT pattern tunic with slashed pockets in the skirts and others wore tunics with dark green collars until the end of the war. Some officers of General rank were known to have preferred gold embroidery rather than the regulation silvered aluminium and their jackets frequently had bright metal buttons.

Three captured SS men in 1944. The two on the left wear the 1940 Army pattern field grey blouse while the man on the right wears the tunic of the camouflaged suit but with field grey service trousers. However, he wears shoulder straps on the tunic which was not officially permitted. Note absence of badges on his cap, and on collar of left hand man (IWM-B10166).

Black leather U-Boat clothing

Members of armoured and reconnaissance regiments of 12. "Hitlerjugend" Division are known to have been issued with Italian black leather submarine clothing during the Normandy campaign. Photographs reveal that both jackets and trousers were worn. The former had a very low standing collar five aluminium buttons down a single-breasted front, two side pockets and a slash pocket with an oblong flap in the left breast. Black leather headdress with black fur linings was worn by some men while others wore either the field grey peaked cap or the black version of the 'ship'-shaped field service cap.

Shirt Sleeve Order

In hot summer weather officers could discard their heavy uniform coats and wear only their grey shirts. Ties were not worn and the shirts could be seen with either an open neck or buttoned neck and with the sleeves rolled up. When the Knight's Cross was worn the shirt collar was worn buttoned. There were no facilities for wearing the shoulder cords with the shirt although photographs do show that a few officers appear to have sewn their shoulder cords on to the shirt for quick identification of their rank. The national emblem sleeve eagle was usually sewn to the left sleeve. Some officers had the sleeve rank badges (intended for camouflage clothing) on the sleeves of shirts worn in shirt sleeve order. The grey uniform shirt had a patch pocket with scalloped flap on each each breast.

47

The Overcoat

The SS-VT wore a black overcoat with the black tunic and breeches. This was a double breasted garment with a deep folded down collar and six buttons in each of two rows down the front. The back had a half belt with two buttons and there was a vent to the waist which could be closed by four small buttons concealed in a pleat. The grey overcoat subsequently issued was the same pattern and had a dark green collar. General officers had grey lapels and wore their collars open with the lapels folded back.

By 1941 most Waffen-SS personnel were wearing the Army pattern field grey greatcoat with either the dark green or grey collars. Collar patches were worn on the greatcoat as were shoulder straps or cords and cuff titles. Many officers wore greatcoats without the collar patches and in some cases deep fur collars were substituted for the normal type of collar. The uniform belt was worn over the greatcoat by the officers, NCOs and men.

Drivers of horse-drawn and other vehicles were issued with a loose surcoat to wear over the overcoat. Basically the same pattern as the overcoat most types had two vertical pockets placed on either side of the breast above the side pockets. These coats were often lined with heavy woollen material. Photographs of men of "Leibstandarte Adolf Hitler" in Poland in the winter of 1939-1940 show sentries wearing almost ankle length sheepskin coats (pelt inside) with a very deep folded down fur collar.

Anoraks and Snow Clothing

Anoraks were either white and lined with fur, field grey, tan coloured or made in reversible white and camouflaged material. They were worn with heavy waterproof trousers and locally made heavy snow boots which were felt lined.

A single-breasted snow smock was also worn. A thigh-length coat, it had an efficient deep hood and face mask. It was buttoned down the breast by five toggle buttons. It had breast pockets and buttoned cuffs.

Many other types of locally produced winter clothing was taken into use in Russia including several types of caps made from pelts with flaps to cover the ears.

SS pattern overcoat in black or grey, showing alternative collar patterns.

SS pattern surcoat for vehicle drivers.

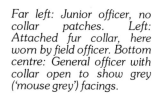

Far left: Junior officer, no collar patches. Left: Attached fur collar, here worn by field officer. Bottom centre: General officer with collar open to show grey ('mouse grey') facings.

Below: Front and back views of SS-VT trooper of Standarte Nr.1 Deutschland" showing black overcoat and shoulder cord.

Camouflaged clothing (Tarnbekleidung)

The most unique and important aspect of uniform development by the Waffen-SS was their almost universal use of camouflaged uniform clothing. The effects of the SS development of this form of dress was to have unprecedented ramifications on the design of military dress and today most armies of the world use green, grey, brown and tan mottled clothing for combat duties much of which owes its ancestry to the original camouflaged smocks first taken into use by the SS-VT units during the Polish campaign of 1939.

Infantry and cavalry smocks, helmet covers, caps, winter anoraks and later even complete suits comprising lightweight camouflaged drill versions of the heavier serge grey uniform were used in the field. Special camouflaged snipers' suits were designed and specially designed camouflaged suits for tank crews including one-piece overalls for self-propelled and other artillery units were introduced in the later phases of the war.

Smocks and helmet covers were made in reversible material with mainly green, or brown, mottled or even leaf patterns which enabled the troops to adapt to the terrain in which they were fighting and the particular season of the year. The most widely used garment was the smock. This had no collar and was laced up the front to fasten at the neck with drawstrings. The cuffs were elasticated (later buttoned) and the thigh length garment had slits in the sides of the breasts to allow the wearer to thrust his hand through to the blouse or jacket beneath. Some versions had drawstrings at the waist, others were elasticated in the same fashion as the cuffs. In most models loops were sewn into the breasts and sleeves to facilitate the fixing of pieces of fern, grass or twigs. Later versions had side pockets with small plastic buttons. The skirt of the smock was sometimes rolled up to make it shorter. Because shoulder straps were not worn on most of this camouflage and indeed on most winter clothing, drill uniforms, and tropical kit, the Waffen-SS had to develop the system being used by the Luftwaffe and Army of identifying the wearer by an arm badge. In the early months of 1943 a system of bars and oak leaves was introduced which were worn on the left upper arm about 10cm from the shoulder. For the General officer ranks the badges were golden yellow on black; for other officers and NCOs they were bright green on black.

The Waffen-SS were ordered not to wear other badges on their camouflaged clothing once these badges were approved but many continued to do so and even wore the sleeve eagle. Army and Italian army camouflaged uniform was also worn by some units, especially in the later part of the war. For the steel helmet cover and camouflaged einheitsmütze, see the section on head wear. The colour plates show the most common camouflage patterns.

SS-VT and Waffen-SS camouflage smock.

Below: camouflage smock and helmet cover in normal use. The NCO is firing a Mauser Pistole Mod. 32 automatic.

Front and rear view of officers wearing the standard issue camouflage smock over service dress. Officer facing camera has the cuff ends tucked back under the elasticated wrist bands, and the skirt of the smock tucked back and held by the belt at waist level, both quite common variations of wearing the garment. He has an Army pattern belt. The other officer has the cuffs and skirt fully visible.

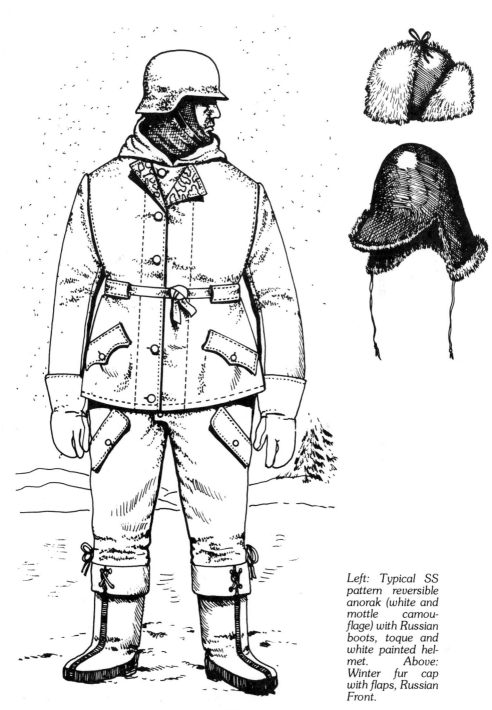

Left: Typical SS pattern reversible anorak (white and mottle camouflage) with Russian boots, toque and white painted helmet. Above: Winter fur cap with flaps, Russian Front.

Motorcyclist special clothing

Waffen-SS motorcyclists and personnel in motorcycle combinations wore field grey rubberised fabric coats. The garment was double-breasted and had two vertical pockets in the sides of the long skirts. There was a pleated yoke to protect the shoulders and the coat was made with a belt and with loose sleeves which buttoned close at the wrist. The long skirts were made to hook back. The gloves worn with this coat were thick leather with a thumb and forefinger. Some officers wore this coat as a waterproof raincoat. Motorcyclists were issued with goggles with wide elasticated straps which were pushed up on the helmet or around the neck when not in use. Officially personal equipment was to be worn under this coat but photographs reveal that many men wore the belt with cartridge pouches over the coat.

Feldgendarmerie

Field police of the Waffen-SS wore the same uniform as the other personnel of the unit plus a special orange embroidered eagle and oak leaf wreath arm badge in lieu of the Waffen-SS sleeve eagle together with an additional cuff title lettered "Feldgendarmerie" in German Gothic script of "SS-Feldgendarmerie" in Roman lettering. This cuff title was worn above the divisional cuff title. On duty they wore a special ringkragen (gorget) suspended on an aluminium chain. The gorget had two bosses, a large eagle and swastika and a grey scroll lettered "Feldgendarmerie" all treated with luminous paint, as illustrated on page 33.

Waffen-SS mountain troops

Mountain Rifle Regiments and all other Mountain support troops wore an oval black badge bearing a white embroidered Edelweiss with yellow stamen on the right upper sleeve of the field blouse and overcoat. An Edelweiss badge was also worn on the left side of the field cap and the mountain cap, the latter becoming the universal field service cap later in the war and known as the 'Einheitsmütze'.

As part of the development of the specialist SS-Mountain Divisions crack alpine guides from the mountainous districts of Bavaria and Austria were recruited and given distinctive badges.

Trained in advanced mountain warfare techniques at the Mountain Warfare Schools they wore regulation mountain troop uniform and waffenfarbe but with the addition of a special breast badge. This comprised an oval 55mm high and 43mm wide black cloth badge embroidered with a 2mm wide aluminium cord edge. In the centre was a 33mm (42mm with stalk) aluminium embroidered Edelweiss with gold wire stamen and the lettering "BERGFÜHRER" (mountain leader) in aluminium wire in a half circle beneath the flower. In winter guides wore climbing socks and mountain pattern boots and, in summer, shirt sleeves with short pumphosen (leather shorts).

Waffen-SS mountain troops forage cap — gebirgsmütze or einheitsmütze.

Waffen-SS mountain troops edelweiss arm badges.

Waffen-SS mountain troops edelweiss cap badge.

SS-Mountain Divisions, special badges. Left to right: Edelweiss worn on upper right arm. Edelweiss cap badge worn on left side of bergmütze. SS pattern national emblem worn on left arm.

Generaloberst Rendulie, the Finnish Oberfelshaber of the German Army on the Finnish Front, with an SS-Obersturmführer of a mountain unit. The general is wearing a green net face mask over his cap. This was a standard issue as an insect repellent.

Service boot

Officer's riding boot

Ankle boot

Mountain boot

Boots

The original footwear of the Bereitschaften and the SS-VT was the calf length heavy leather boot also worn by the Army and Luftwaffe. These boots were worn in specially tapered trousers. Later ankle boots made without toe caps were also taken into use.

Mountain rifle regiments wore proper climbing boots with specially designed cleated soles with mountaineering studs. Calf length webbing gaiters were also used by these soles with mountaineering studs. Ankle-length webbing gaiters were also used by these specialist divisions.

SS Officers usually wore knee length black boots. Mounted units and senior officers wore these boots with nickel plated spurs worn on straps buckled across the instep.

Personal Equipment

The SS-VT and Waffen-SS wore a black leather waistbelt with a special buckle. The officers' buckle was the locket and clasp type and the buckle for the NCOs and other ranks was rectangular.

The original pouches were the M1909 pattern. In the various orders of combat dress, two pouches were carried on either side of the buckle. Each pouch was split into three, each section containing ten rounds of rifle ammunition. The waistbelt was 4.5cm wide and was made to slide through loops at the rear of each pouch the centre one of which was fitted with a steel 'D' ring through which the braces were looped. The bayonet and the entrenching tool were suspended from frogs on the waistbelt and on the left side. In 1939 the bayonet was being carried over the entrenching tool and suspended by a loop to the entrenching tool's frog. Later it was worn in its own frog in front of the entrenching tool. The M1934 haversack was hung from two loops at the right hip and on it, suspended from a steel 'D' ring, and retained by a strap which passed through a loop on the haversack flap was the M1931 water bottle with its oval cup secured over the mouthpiece.

The anti-gas respirator in its cylindrical fluted lightweight metal container was carried on a web strap over the right shoulder the cylinder lying at an angle on the left hip. The bottom attachment to the container was usually hooked to the rear of the belt.

The new pattern braces issued in 1939 consisted of two 4cm wide tapered black straps which passed over the shoulders from the 'D' rings on the central pouches and were joined with a steel ring to the 2.5cm wide back strap which descended to fasten to the waistbelt at centre back. There were two large steel 'D' rings fitted to the shoulder straps from which the assault pack or the rucksack could be fitted.

A lightweight web yoke could be fitted to the braces from which the assault pack;

Left: Rectangular white metal belt buckle worn by NCOs and other ranks. Right Officer's clasp and locket type belt buckle.

worn in light field order, could be worn. Full marching order consisted of the M1939 pack mentioned above complete with tent quarter, greatcoat, blankets and clothing bag.

Special pouches were issued concurrently with new weapons, including the MP 43 and MP 44 and the SG 44. These pouches were usually webbing and were carried on the waist belt, diagonally to make withdrawal easier.

Mountain rifle (jäger) regiments were issued with special mountaineering rucksacks and carried larger capacity waterbottles. They also carried various specialised climbing gear including ropes, ice axes, crampons, and in some cases skis, and wore special climbing boots.

The cavalry wore their equipment mainly suspended from the waistbelt and were provided with braces which had no yoke fitting. Engineers and Artillery were provided with special rucksacks to provide facilities for their unique functions. The former wore large pouches attached to the fronts of their waistbelts to carry detonators, oval grenades and fuses. These pouches had pouches for rifle ammunition fitted to their sides. The Engineers knapsack carried specialised detonating and smoke equipment. Medical Orderlies carried special pouches on their waistbelts for dressings and other medical supplies.

Personal Weapons

The M 98 and M 43 pattern rifles were carried and later the MP 38, 40, MP 43 and its 43/1, the MP 44 and the St. G. 44. Officers and NCOs carried either the P 08 or the P36 pistol in a black leather holster, officers carrying these weapons or smaller automatic pistols such as the Walther PPK.

The Tent Quarter

This ingenious piece of equipment known in German as the 'Zeltbahn' was a piece of camouflaged (Waffen-SS pattern) waterproof material cut in a triangle with a slit in the material through which the head could pass. It served as a windbreak and could be joined to the three other quarters carried by comrades to form a good tent. On other occasions it served as a poncho and was worn in a variety of ways, the material acting as half-sleeves, or could be rolled to leave the arms free.

The Zeltbahn (tent quarter) being worn in 1940 by a member of Standarte "Germania". The man beyond wears the camouflaged smock.

Below: Scale drawing of zeltbahn (shelter quarter). Bottom: Methods of using and folding.

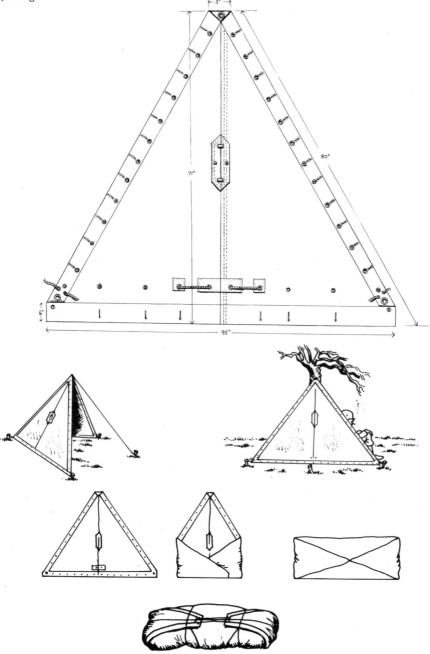

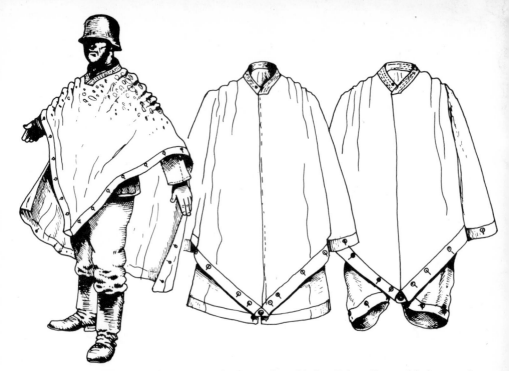

Above: Methods of donning and wearing the zeltbahn. Below: Four zeltbahn joined to make a bivouac. Note man second left wearing field grey and white reversible anorak (IWM-BU5395).

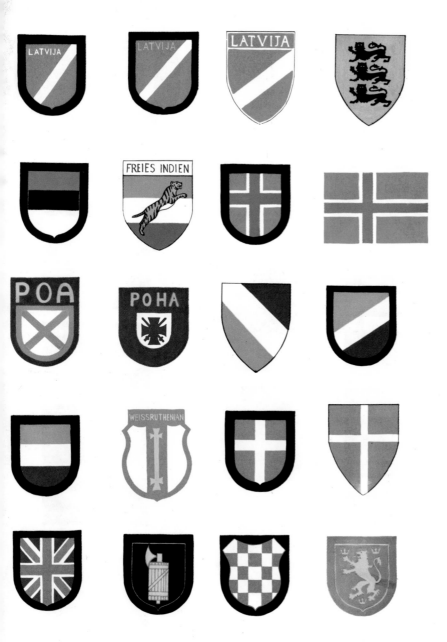

National legion and volunteer arm badges. Left to right, top to bottom: Latvia (three variants), Estonia (Nordland), Estonia, Free Indian, Norway (two variants), Vlasov (Russia Nr. 1), Kaminsky, Holland, Holland (Fr. Leg. Nederland), Holland, Russian Nr. 2, Denmark (two variants), Legion of St. George, Italy, Croatia, Galicia.

Top, left to right, two rows: France (Army pattern, also worn by Waffen-SS), France, Belgium (Army pattern), Belgium, Albania, Flanders (Legion Flandern), Italy, Italy (Army pattern), Holland (variant). *Waffen-SS rank badges for camouflage clothing,* top to bottom, left to right, three rows: Oberstgruppenführer, Obergruppenführer, Gruppenführer, Brigadeführer, Oberführer, Standartenführer, Obersturmbannführer, Sturmbannführer, Hauptsturmführer, Obersturmführer, Untersturmführer, Sturmscharführer, (Hauptscharführer 4 stripes, Oberscharführer 3 stripes, not shown), Scharführer, Unterscharführer. All badges in colour plates about half actual size.

As this picture shows, infantry troops in the attack generally travelled as lightly as possible. The men of an assault platoon of Standarte "Germania" in May 1940 are wearing waistbelts, ammunition, pouches, anti-gas respirators and anti-gas capes clipped to the straps of the respirator containers. Nearest man has his camouflage smock tucked into his belt. Grenades, ammunition boxes, and MG 34 tripod are also being carried by men in this group.

The same group of men from Standarte "Germania" as shown on the previous page. The Unterscharführer (right) has his smock hanging with his small pack from the waistbelt at the rear, while the Sturmmann (left) has his at the front. Note absence of collar patches.

SS-VT Black Service Dress

After the outbreak of war it was unusual to see Waffen-SS troops in the black service clothing although some officers may have worn it on furlough or on special ceremonial occasions. Before the war, the "Leibstandarte", the SS-VT Standarten and Sturmbanne, the Staffs of the Academies, and the SS-Totenkopfstandarte all wore the black service uniform for special parade and ceremonial duties. In addition the "Leibstandarte" were issued in 1937 with special white parade equipment which included white belts, cartridge pouches and shoulder braces.

The black uniform comprised the peaked cap (Tellermütze), the undress field service cap (worn off-duty in the barracks, etc.), the service tunic, breeches and high boots. Field Officers wore steel nickel plated spurs. The brown shirt was worn with black tie by the NCOs and enlisted men and white shirts were worn by the officers.

In 1937 officers were provided with field grey cloth dress belts which were faced with an aluminium woven fabric with a woven-in SS rune design. The belt had two slides on either side of the buckle. These slides were also faced with the silver coloured fabric and they and the belt had two woven-in black silk stripes along either edge. The buckle was the special SS officers pattern. Officers wore white gloves with gauntlet cuffs and white short gloves with the black overcoat. Some photographs show officers wearing brown leather gloves. NCOs wore short white gloves. Other ranks wore short white gloves on special occasions. Officers wore an aluminium cord aigullette under the right shoulder cord and fastened to a small hook under the right lapel.

Officers and Warrant Class NCOs carried swords. The swords were carried in the same manner as in the old German Army, that is to say, on a thin canvas belt worn under the coat with only one suspender and hook. The sword was suspended on one ring the suspender strap emerging through a slit in the left tunic pocket. The swords had bright nickel plated knuckle bow guards and black grips bound with aluminium wire. The scabbards were black enamelled metal. The officers' swords had a black roundel on each side of the grip, edged with silver and bearing the silver SS runes. The NCOs had their runes on the flat top of the pommel. The tops of the officers' scabbards had a silver interlaced design. Mounted troops carried sabres when on foot. The swords were carried on the saddle when they were mounted.

SS sword knots were made of aluminium wire and had an aluminium woven fabric strap with two interwoven black silk stripes on either side. The stem of the knot had a black silk roundel with the black SS runes in the centre. The NCO's sword knot straps were black with three interwoven aluminium stripes. Junior NCOs had black and aluminium sabre knots or bayonet knots (troddeln). The troopers' bayonet knots or sabre knots were aluminium but had stems in the colour of the squadron or company, red, blue, green, yellow or white.

From 1933 the Allgemeine-SS and the SS-VT and SS-TV were entitled to carry the SS ceremonial dagger (dolch). They were permitted to wear this weapon in most orders of dress except on parade when the sword, sabre of rifle and bayonet were carried. Officers and senior NCOs are known to have worn the dagger on occasions (eg, at weddings or official receptions) during the war years.

The dagger was shaped like a Gothic hunting knife and had a black wooden grip with a white metal national emblem and a roundel with the SS runes. The sheath was made of black enamelled metal and had nickelled mounts. On the polished blade the words of the SS motto "MEINE EHRE HEIST TREUE" was etched in Gothic upper

67

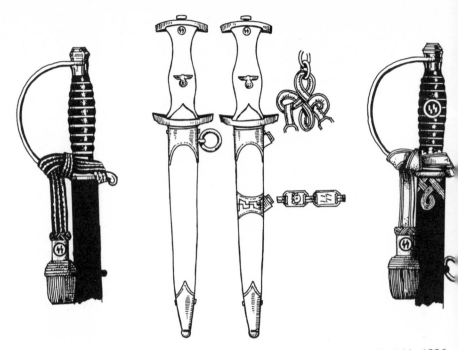

Left to right: Senior NCO's pattern sword, SS ceremonial dagger (Dolch), 1936 pattern special dagger and suspension for officers and NCOs, officer's pattern sword.

and lower case lettering. The dagger was suspended on a short black leather strap.

In 1936 a special dagger was issued to the officers and NCOs who had been in the SS since 1933. It was similar to the 1933 model, but the new sheath had an additional fitting around the centre with a continuous swastika design. This special dagger had a suspender consisting of a series of linked oblong plates alternatively decorated with SS runes and deathsheads.

Bands

SS bands were formed for each regiment. Each battalion had its own Corps of Drums. On the march the Banks of Music were led by the Corps of Drums. The Corps of Drums was commanded and led by the Drum Major, as in the Army and the band was directed by the Bandmaster or Director of Music. Bands and the Corps of Drums wore the same black uniform as the men of the regiment or battalion with the addition of wings (Schwalbennestern) worn on the shoulder of the coat. The wings were black and were decorated with seven vertical bars of aluminium lace and were edged with the same. In addition the bandsmen had a 3cm long aluminium fringing on their wings.

The Corps of Drums had shallow brass shelled drums with white rims decorated with black equilateral triangles (flat side along the outer edge). Behind the Drums and

Fifes and at the head of the band marched the splendid Schellenbaumträger. The designs of these elaborate instruments were varied from regiment to regiment. The Drum Major had wings with 7cm long fringing, wore gauntlet gloves and carried an NCO's pattern sword. His silver headed mace had aluminium and black silk twisted cords.

Cavalry units had mounted Trumpet Corps led by a Kettle Drummer. The kettle drums banners were black with aluminium trimming and were made in the panelled style used by the cavalry of the old German Army. Each panel had the national emblem and the deathshead plus some regimental inscription. The trumpeters, usually mounted on greys, had silver trumpets with banners of black cloth with aluminium fringing and with aluminium deathsheads on one side and the SS runes plus the national emblem or some regimental title on the other. The trumpets had aluminium and black silk twisted cords and long tassels.

After the outbreak of war band personnel also wore field grey uniform but with the bandsmen's distinctions noted above.

The Corps of Drums and military band of a VT "Totenkopf" Standarte in black parade dress.

Top: March past in 1939 by "Leibstandarte Adolf Hitler" (LAH) in the distinctive white leather equipment issued only to this regiment. Above: Honour guard of a SS-VT Standarte in 1937, black parade dress with overcoats; note black leather equipment.

A fine view of the smartly turned out honour guard of SS-VT Standarte Nr. 1 "Deutschland" at Munich in October 1938 for the arrival of British Prime Minister Chamberlain. Black parade dress with white shirts and white gloves.

Hitler at the Nuremberg Rally of 1938. On the left are two drum majors, one from the band of SS-VT "Leibstandarte Adolf Hitler", and the colour party on the right is probably also from "LAH", before white equipment was issued to the whole regiment aside from the band.

Waffen-SS School of Music

The permanent staff of the school — "SS-Musik-Schule-Braunschweig" — wore the SS runes on the right collar patch together with a cuff title lettered "Musikschule Braunschweig" in Roman upper and lower case. Students wore a special grey embroidered lyre badge on both collar patches and had a Gothic cypher on both shoulder straps. They also wore the school cuff title. Students wore the army pattern field blouse with dark green collars.

SS-Fallschirmjäger

Men of this arm wore standard Army pattern infantry field blouse and trousers with ankle boots and gaiters. Jump clothing comprised a special pattern parachutist's smock made in Army camouflaged material plus the Luftwaffe pattern parachutists' helmet. Some photographs show the helmet being worn with nets, or without. No devices appear to have been carried on the sides. The SS pattern waistbelt was worn over the smock. Apart from the special parachute clothing and the appropriate cuff title, SS-Fallschirmjäger followed entirely the uniform style of other contemporary Waffen SS units. Some smocks may have been made from SS pattern camouflage material.

Unterscharführer of the Waffen-SS Fallschirmjäger in field grey service dress but wearing the lightweight parachutist helmet. Note the cuff title "1".

73

SS-Specialist Troops

In 1942 specialist personnel known as 'Fachführer' were introduced for the Waffen-SS to correspond to the 'Sonderführer' of the Army. They were distinguished by a special red and light grey waffenfarbe which comprised a twisted cord around the shoulder strap with two red to every six grey twists and special diamond-shaped sleeve badges. The Sonderführer of the Army wore circular badges on the lower right arm, the Fachführer of the SS wore their diamond badges on the left sleeve just above the cuff title. It is likely that they had plain black right collar patches. There were some instances (from pictorial evidence) that Army pattern Sonderführer badges were worn on occasion, probably due to shortage of Waffen-SS badges. The diamond sleeve badges are illustrated:

First row from left to right:
SS-HQ Replacement and recruitment.
Nationality Work Groups.
Administration SS Economic HQ.

Second row:
Administration SS Agricultural Economic HQ.
Administration SS Economic Management HQ.
SS-Commissiarat for Nationality.

Third row:
SS-Race and Resettlement HQ.
SS-Press and War Economy Group.
SS-Reich Security.

Fourth row:
SS-Judge Advocate Officers.
SS-Administrative Staff.
SS-Armourer NCOs.

Fifth row:
Farriers of Waffen-SS Reiter Regiments.
SS-Technical Officers.
SS-Signallers.

Sixth row:
SS-Veterinary Staff.
SS-Doctors and Dentists.
SS-Medical Orderlies.

Seventh row:
SS-SecrSS-Security Staff (not strictly Waffen-SS).
SS-Transport NCOs.
SS-Bandmasters.

Cuff titles of 9. Pz-Gren. Regt. "Nordland" and 10. Pz -Gren. Regt. "Westland" shows the most common style of lettering.

Cuff Titles

Officers and men of the Waffen-SS wore a 28mm wide band of black ribbon around the top edge of the left cuff. The black strip was edged with 2mm aluminium stripes or grey silk. The cuff titles worn by the SS-VT and Waffen-SS are listed below. This is not a complete listing, but includes all the most important units.

SS-VT

Regiment or Unit	Lettering	Style
"Leibstandarte"	Adolf Hitler	autograph.
Standarte "Deutschland"	Deutschland	Gothic upper and lower case*.
Standarte "Germania"	Germania	Gothic upper and lower case*.
Standarte "Der Führer"	Der Führer	Gothic upper and lower case*.
"SS-Nachrichtensturmbann"	Full title	Gothic upper and lower case.
"SS-Pioniersturmbann"	Full title	Gothic upper and lower case.
"SS-Schule Tölz"	Full title	Gothic upper and lower case.
"SS-Schule Braunschweig"	Full title	(1) Gothic upper and lower case.
		(2) Gothic script.
"SS-Verwaltungsschule"	Full title	Gothic upper and lower case.
"SS-Ärtzliche Akademie"	Full title	Gothic upper and lower case.

*At first the three battalions of each of these regiments were identified by the coloured stripes along the edges of their cuff titles, which were (I) green, (II) blue and (III) red respectively.

Waffen-SS Divisions

Division	Legend and style
1st.	"Adolf Hitler" — autograph.
2nd.	"Das Reich" — roman upper and lower case. "Deutschland", "Germania" and "Der Führer" as before.
3rd.	A deathshead symbol; or "Totenkopf", "Thule" and "Theodore Eicke" all in Roman upper and lower case.
4th.	"SS-Polizei-Division" in both Gothic and Roman upper and lower case.
5th.	"Wiking", "Germania", "Westland" and "Nordland" in upper and lower case Roman or Gothic.
6th.	"Nord", "Michael Gassmair" and "Reinhard Heydrich" in Roman upper and lower case. Note that "Gassmair" has the German double "s".
7th.	"Prinz Eugen" in Roman upper and lower case.
8th.	"SS-Kavallerie Division" in Gothic upper and lower and "Florian Geyer" in Roman upper and lower case.
9th.	"Hohenstaufen" in Roman upper and lower case.
10th.	"Frundsberg" in Roman upper and lower case.
11th.	"Nordland", "Norge", "Danmark" and "Herman von Salza" all in Roman upper and lower case.
12th.	"Hitlerjugend" in autograph form and in Roman upper and lower case.
13th.	None.

Division	Legend and style
14th.	None.
15th.	None.
16th.	"Reichführer-SS" in Roman upper and lower case.
17th.	"Götz von Berlichingen" in Roman upper and lower case.
18th.	"Horst Wessel" in Roman upper and lower case.
19th.	None.
20th.	None.
21st.	"Skanderbeg" in Roman upper and lower case.
22nd.	None.
23rd.	"Nederland", "General Seyffardt" and De Ruiter" (also "De Ruyter") all in Roman upper and lower case.
24th.	None.
25th.	None.
26th.	None.
27th.	"Langemarck" in Roman upper and lower case.
28th.	"Wallonien" in Roman upper and lower case. "Wallonie" also known in Gothic upper and lower case.
29th.	"Italien" in Roman upper and lower case not authenticated.
30th.	None.
31st.	None.
32nd.	"30. Januar" in Roman upper and lower case.
33rd.	"Charlemagne" in Roman upper and lower case.
34th.	"Landstorm Nederland" in Roman upper and lower case.
35th.	None.
36th.	"Dirlewanger" in Roman upper and lower case not authenticated.
37th.	None.
38th.	None. Members may have worn cuff titles of former school or unit.

Name	Legend and Style
Denmark	"Freikorps Danmark" in Roman upper and lower case.
Flanders	"Frw. Legion Flandern" in Roman upper and lower case.
Norway	"Legion Norwegen" in Roman upper and lower case.
Holland	"Frw. Legion Niederland" in Roman upper and lower case.
Finland	"Finnisches Frw. Bataillon der Waffen-SS" in Roman upper and lower case.
Britain	"Britisches Freikorps" in Roman upper and lower case.
Serbia	None
India	None.
Turkey	"Östturkischer Waffen-Verband der SS" in Roman upper and lower case.
Danzig	"SS-Heimwehr Danzig" in Gothic. "D" in Danzig only upper case letter.

Field Police

Two types known, one reading "Feldgendarmerie" in Gothic upper and lower case. The other "SS-Feldgendarmerie" in Roman upper and lower case.

War Correspondents
"SS-KB-Abtl." in Roman upper and lower case.
"SS-Kriegsberichter" in Roman upper and lower case and "Kurt Eggers" in Roman upper and lower case. Worn above the divisional cuff title.

SS Parachutist Units
"Fallschirmjäger" in Roman upper and lower case. "SS-Fallschirmjäger" also alleged to have been worn.

National sleeve emblems for Finland (right) and Norway (Hird). See also the colour plates.

Flags and Standards

The regimental standards were of the 'Vexillum' pattern and consisted of a red, rectangular banner, bearing the white circle and black swastika in the centre suspended from a bar beneath a black, silver edged box on which the name of the unit was emblazoned. The standard and box was carried on a staff at the head of which (above the title box) was a metal wreath of oak leaves bound with gilded ribbons in which a black metal swastika was set. Above the wreath at the head of the staff, was a gilded metal eagle with its wings half outstretched (as if to take off). Red, white and black twisted woollen cords were attached to the sides of the title box and were then looped around the ends of the horizontal pole with heavy tassels pendant on either side. This type of standard is known to have been carried by the pre-war "LAH" the "Deutschland", "Germania" and "Der Führer" and "Totenkopf" Regiments.

Each battalion of the regiment carried its own flat (Fahnen). These comprised a rectangular red field with a large white circle in the centre and the black swastika emblazoned in the centre of that. The flag was attached to the staff by six aluminium rings and trimmed on the three other sides by a fringe of black and aluminium threads. In the top corner next to the staff was a small black patch, edged with aluminium cord which was emblazoned with the battalion's identification:— "I/SS"; "II/SS" and "III/SS" (all the SS lettering being Sig-runes) for the "LAH" and for Regiment "Germania" — "I/SS2"; "II/SS2" and "III/SS2", etc.

A Standard Party consisted of the Standartenträger (Standard Bearer) who was always a Senior NCO flanked by two officers known as Standartenführeren. The Standard Bearer wore a black bandolier over the left shoulder. It was edged with a 4cm wide bright aluminium lace. The leather socket of the bandolier for both the standard and the flag was normally positioned on the bearer's right hip level with the edge of his tunic.

On parade the Standard Bearer wore a gorget, made of polished aluminium, bearing the national emblem, and suspended on two large bosses emblazoned with the SS runes. It was carried on a neck chain consisting of links alternatively embossed with SS runes and deathsheads. In both the black and field grey uniform the Standard Bearers wore white gauntlet gloves.

79

Divisional Badges

Divisional signs were displayed at the front and the rear of vehicles and were generally stencilled on to the bodywork in white or yellow paint. Sometimes other colours (eg, red) were used to indicate corps command, etc. Signs were used with or without the enclosing shields. Variations appeared at intervals and these are noted. However in the later stages of the war when resources became restricted many vehicles omitted to carry signs although the designs can often be confirmed from military signposting. Some signs had heraldic significance. Note for example the badge of 1. Panzer Division which used a symbol which was connected with its commander Sepp Dietrich. The word "Dietrich" is German for picklock or skeleton key. The wreath was probably introduced to commemorate the award to Dietrich of the Oak leaves to his Knight's Cross. In the signs on pages 81 to 83, read across each of the rows from left to right, with the book turned sideways.

Page 81
First Row
1st Div. until 1942; SS Panzer Korps 1943; 12th. Div. 1943-1944; 1st. Div. from 1942; 2nd. Div.; 2nd. Div. in use until 1944; 2nd. Div. variant in use until 1944.
Second Row
3rd. Div.; 4th. Div.; 4th. Div., variant in bright green, in use before 1944; 5th. Div.; 6th. Div.; 6th. Div. variant.
Third Row
7th. Div.; 7th. Div., variant; 8th. Div.; 9th. Div.; 9th. Div., variant; light blue on yellow; 9th. Div., variant after Arnhem 1944 — red windmill.
Page 82
First Row
10th. Div.; 10th. Div., variant white on a yellow ground; 11th. Div., variant; 11th Div.; 12th. Div.
Second Row
13th. Div.; 13th. Div., variant; 14th. Div.; 14th. Div., variant unconfirmed; 15th. Div.; 16th. Div.
Third Row
17th. Div.; 18th. Div.; 18th. Div., variant; 19th. Div.; 20th. Div.; 21st. Div.
Page 83
First Row
22nd. Div.; 23rd. Div.; 24th. Div.; 25th. Div.; 26th. Div.; 27th. Div.
Second Row
28th. Div.; 28th. Div., variant; 29th. Div.; 30th. Div.; 31st. Div., variant; 32nd. Div.
Third Row
33rd. Div.; 34th. Div.; 35th. Div.; 36th. Div.; 37th. Div.; 38th. Div.

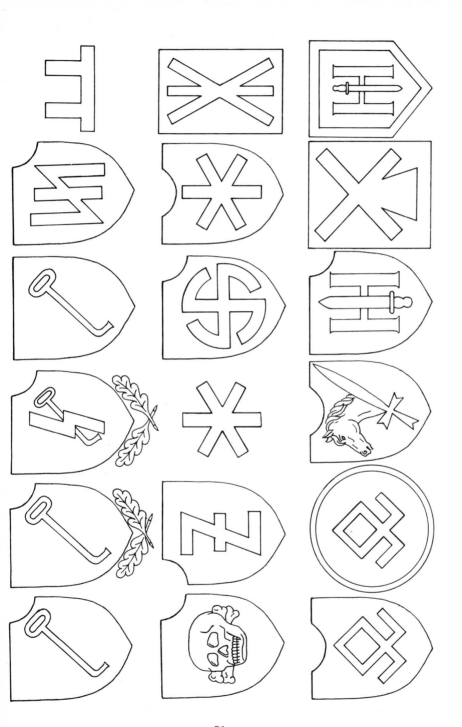

Left: Two more divisional badges; 8th. Div., variant (left) and 31st. Div. Below: Norwegian volunteers of SS "Freiwilligen Legion Norwegen". Note the national colours below the arm badge. Man on left has collar patches and cuff title while man on right has neither.

Pictorial Section

On the following pages we present a selection of photographs, in some cases previously unpublished, which show many aspects of the uniforms and equipment of the SS-VT and Waffen-SS in the 1937-45 period. These supplement the text, drawings, and other illustrations in the main body of the book and give an idea of the huge variation there was in uniform matters as far as the armed SS units were concerned.

Rottenführer showing regulation positioning of arm badges and cuff title ("Heimwehr Danzig"). Note helmet camouflage bands.

Top: Two Waffen-SS artillerymen in 1942 wearing the Army pattern field grey service dress and basic equipment — belt, bayonet and scabbard, ammunition pouches, and anti-gas respirator. Left: SS-Sturmann wearing camouflaged cap, field grey service dress, slip-on cypher 'R' on the shoulder strap, and camouflaged forage cap. Note the SS ring on his finger, shown in close-up above.

Above: A 8cm heavy mortar team of 4. "Polizei" Division in June 1940. Note the police pattern collar patches and the police insignia on the helmets of two of the men. The SS pattern national emblem is worn on the left arm (WM-MH1906). *Right:* The camouflaged version of the special panzer clothing tunic worn by a Waffen-SS panzer-grenadier over his field grey service tunic at Tarnopol, April 1944. Note the full equipment and braces worn, and the method of suspending grenades.

Above: Light machine gun team in May 1940 wearing the then newly issued camouflage smock and helmet cover. Note how it was cut loose enough at the back to be worn over the pack, as here (IWM-MH1923). Right: SS pattern reversible winter anorak, white on one side, camouflaged on the other, and with hood and five-button front.

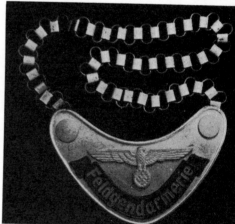

Left: SS-Brigadeführer Paul Kanstein in the field grey version of the black dress tunic. Top: Officer on right wears the tunic of the camouflaged suit but field grey trousers and einheitsmütze. Officer on left has the later pattern smock with lower pockets and wears the officer's field service cap; 1944 period. Above: Gorget and suspension chain of the Feldgendarmerie. Also worn by the SS-Feldgendarmerie.

Top: Motorcyclist crews of a reconnaissance unit wearing the rubberised waterproof coat. Above: Member of SS "Poleizi" Division wearing camouflage smock and 1939 pattern SS forage cap with police insignia instead of SS insignia. Right: The 1942 pattern field blouse worn both outside and inside the trousers by these members of 12. "Hitler Jugend" Division in 1944. Note gaiters and ankle boots.

This *Unterscharführer* holds the specialist qualification of *Bergführer* though his breast badge denoting this is obscured in this view. He is acting as an instructor in a SS mountain warfare school and is demonstrating crampons and the use of the ice axe. He wears the service dress of mountain troops with the usual Army pattern field grey service dress and SS insignia, June 1943.

The celebrated tank commander Michael Wittman and his crew pose in front of their Tiger tank wearing the all black special tank clothing, with black forage caps and insignia. Note that Wittman wears the officer's pattern field grey service cap. Shirts are brown or field grey, ties are black, and the wool gloves are standard issue grey items.

Above: Bass drummer of SS-VT Standarte Nr.2 "Germania" in 1938, wearing the black parade dress. Above, right: Oberscharführer wearing the other ranks' pattern of peaked cap first introduced in 1939 for wear by senior NCOs. Right: The M1944 field blouse, based in cut on the British battle dress blouse, worn by a solder of a SS mountain division in 1945 (IWM-EA65338). Opposite page, lower left: SS-Oberscharführer of 22. SS-Freiwilligen — Kavallerie Division.

Above, left: Unterscharführer musician of 3. SS-Pz. Div. "Totenkopf" wearing field grey service dress with musician's 'swallows nest' and the other ranks' peak cap. Note the early style piping on the collar edge. Above: Officer wearing M1944 field blouse (see lower picture opposite) — note collar patch positions — and 1940 pattern officer's forage cap with aluminium piping. Below: Officer of 7. "Prinz Eugen" Div. (mountain) wearing NCO pattern field service cap with officer's cords (note cloth peak).

This page, above: Two holders of the Knights' Cross (Ritterkreuzträger). An Obersturmbannführer and Sturmbannführer, of the Dutch volunteer division in Russia, March 1944. They wear the reversible anorak and reversible winter trousers — camouflage on left, plain field grey on white. Note hite einheitsmütze and fur cap. Right: Three types of head wear. Note unofficial wearing of edelweiss badge on field service cap of "Viking" division officer. Opposite page, top: infantry in the long winter smock with helmet covers, early 1944. Left: Infantry NCO in winter smock and white trouser covers, late 1943. Right, Personnel of "General Seyffart" Regiment at Narva, 1944, in varied winter gear — anoraks, quilted Army pattern winter suits, etc.

Top: Cossacks of 15.(SS)
Kavallerie Korps, 1944.
Note Army pattern collar
patches. Above: Volunteers
of Legion Niederland. Note
national shield. Right: Ski
troops in Finland, 1943,
wearing one-piece windproof
coveralls and white cap
covers.